I0804713

PotChangers

Innovative Change in an Ever-Changing World

Principles of Leadership for Organizational Effectiveness

Dr. J. Elvin Sadler

SACK PUBLISHING

Body Dynamics Series
G.A.M.E Executive International
Ministry Consultants, Inc.

Cover by Sanctuary Innerprises, LLC, Charlotte, North Carolina

PotChangers:
Innovative Change in an Ever-changing World

ISBN 978-0-578-23743-5 (Print)
ISBN 978-0-578-23742-8 (Digital)

5703 Falkirk Lane
Matthews, North Carolina 28104

KDP Publishing, LLC

Praise for *PotChangers*

"There is nothing like a good meal that is cooked in a pot. Dr. Elvin Sadler prepares a good meal in this riveting book, *PotChangers: Innovative Change in an Ever-Changing World.* This thought-provoking book is an absolutely flawless work that provides a theological and ecclesiological framework for church development and leadership challenges. While there are many factors that will confront the post-pandemic church, this book will provide you with inspiration, guidance, and tools necessary to make the changes and adjustments required for success. This is a must-read and a work suitable for impactful change."

Bishop Sir Walter Mack, pastor and author
Union Baptist Church
Winston- Salem, North Carolina

"Dr. J. Elvin Sadler, in his groundbreaking book, *PotChangers: Innovative Change in an Ever-Changing World,* reveals to us a necessary framework for adaptive change in an ever-changing world. While our personal, professional, and ministry landscapes have changed and are still changing, *PotChangers* offers us timeless tools filled with wisdom principles and practical examples to guide us on an effective path for impactful leadership in a changing world. 'Changing our Pots' is an insightful metaphor for assessing and evaluating the need and time to reset, retool, and renew. *PotChangers* helps us to reevaluate our leadership approaches and styles, as well as the effectiveness of our organizations. *PotChangers* is timely and essential for leaders in any profession. Pastors and ministry team members will grow and become the adaptive leaders your organization needs in these ever-changing times. This is a must-read!"

The Reverend Dr. David M. Nelson
Senior pastor, New Hope Baptist Church, Akron, Ohio
Executive director of Progressive Alliance CDC

"A wonderful opportunity for those who have not had the benefit of Dr. Elvin Sadler's mentoring to glean from his years of leadership experience in this innovative guide for leading organizational change."

The Reverend Dr. Karen Anderson
Senior pastor, First African Methodist Episcopal Church
Las Vegas, Nevada

"In these uncertain times, change can be difficult, even frightening, but it's inevitable. In *PotChangers*, Dr. Sadler shares principles to help you meet the challenges facing leaders in an ever-changing world. After reading Dr. Sadler's work, I am confident you will have the courage and confidence to 'change the Pot.'"

Dr. Brian R. Thompson, senior pastor
Simon Temple A.M.E. Zion Church
Fayetteville, North Carolina

"*PotChangers* is a book for all church leaders. It is filled with practical and godly wisdom for equipping a leader with the knowledge needed to lead change in an organization. Well worth reading."

The Reverend Dr. Matthew Williams, senior pastor
South Union Mennonite Church
West Liberty, Ohio

"*PotChangers* is an impactful book that presents practical and pragmatic ideas for personal progress. This book will challenge the perspective and transform the thinking of the reader for innovative change."

Dr. Theo Johnson, senior pastor
Sweet Home Missionary Baptist Church
Miami, Florida

"In these pages, you will hear Rev. Dr. Sadler's voice of encouragement and wisdom. Dr. Sadler has lived a very full life, and he shares both practical insights and deep spiritual truths that he has learned on his journey. This book is applicable and accessible for pastors and church leaders. Very few books speak to leaders in the pulpit and the pew. I give thanks to God that I've been able to sit under Rev. Dr. Sadler's teaching at United Theological Seminary. I pray he will continue to be a holy change-agent for the Kingdom of God."

The Reverend Dr. Hugh E Hendrickson, pastor
Lavonia First United Methodist Church
Lavonia, Georgia

"Creative, transformational, and cutting edge are just a few words to describe this very insightful, well-crafted work inspired by God. *PotChangers* is a must-read for every pastor who wants to push the envelope of traditional norms to the edge of revealing truths. Dr. Elvin Sadler gives all the tools needed to equip the twenty-first-century church while empowering twenty-second-century saints. He takes years of anointed wisdom, recharged by practical theology, to pour out discerning grace in every chapter. This book, beyond a doubt, will change your ministry forever."

Dr. Anthony Reed, senior pastor
The Purple Church
Miami, Florida

"This is more than a book; it is the perfect tool for the pastoral toolbox. Dr. Elvin Sadler provides both spiritual and realistic insights on how to be an 'effective, innovative change leader' for the church. Every pastor needs to take heed to the wisdom it provides for a proper perspective upon being assigned to a new or first pastoral appointment. *PotChangers* will definitely help you!"

The Reverend William Bert Neal III, D.Min.
Senior pastor, Wesley Chapel United Methodist Church
McDonough, Georgia

"To God be the glory for such an enlightening, timely, and on-point book. Thank you, Dr. Sadler, for your excellent apostolic spirit. Your seasoned level of academia will always be highly appreciated."

Dr. Willie Eugene Marshall
Presiding elder, Ozark-Troy District
African Methodist Episcopal Church

"Open systems are permeable and interact with their environments by sharing ideas, causing them to adapt to change quickly, making them better able to serve the environment, while closed systems resist new ideas, causing them to not only fail in serving their environments, but ultimately lead to their death. In his timely book, *PotChangers: Innovative Change in an Ever-Changing World,* Dr. J. Elvin Sadler lays out the case for all systems—be they corporate, governmental, religious, or otherwise—not only to adapt to their changing environments, but to be the catalyst for their change. Those systems that dare to yield to the vulnerabilities of change by incorporating lessons learned with innovation will find great reward."

The Reverend Dr. Amy S. Ciceron, senior pastor
St. Julia A.M.E. Zion Church
Jacksonville, North Carolina

"*PotChangers* considers how the political, economic, and societal challenges of the present have caused us to change how we process and move information. In light of the realities caused by recent cataclysmic shifts in culture, this book presents a compelling case for the need for organizational innovation while offering practical and time-tested reflections learned from the author's mother. Readers will have their consciousness raised while being encouraged to think more deeply about changes needed for a productive future."

Dr. Rudy Rasmus, pastor
St. John's United Methodist Church
Houston, Texas
Author of *I'm Black, I'm Christian, I'm Methodist*
(Abingdon Press, 2020)

Acknowledgments

This book is presented in honor of all the corporate and spiritual entrepreneurs who blazed the trail of unchartered territory to bring about innovative change in your organizations and ministries. It is also presented in honor of the students in my cohort of the doctoral program of United Theological Seminary, Dayton, Ohio. You thought it not robbery to sit under my tutelage. You helped to perfect my craft and to prove the principles of innovative change.

All of you are the authentic *PotChangers*!

Dedication

This book is dedicated to my parents, DeWitt and Mildred Sadler, who never stifled my ability to dream and grow. It is also dedicated to my siblings, Brenda, Edward, Kenneth, and John, who put up with me and nurtured their baby brother. It is also dedicated to my wife, Stefanie; our children, Leslyn, Courtney, Kiersten, Moncrecia, and Denmar; our sons-in-law, Alexis and J.R.; and our grandchildren, Jishun, Rhylan, Carter, Olivia, and Caysen, who bring tremendous joy to my life. I love you all! And finally, to the One who breathed life and purpose into me. I will forever be grateful for Your grace and mercy. Thank You, Father, for loving me!

Contents

Foreword

Alvin Toffler, author of *Future Shock* and *The Third Wave,* foresaw the challenges facing the church and other institutions when he proposed that "the illiterate of the twenty-first century will be those who cannot learn, unlearn, and relearn"—in other words, those who lack lifelong learning skills and dispositions.

The most effective leaders are lifelong learners who embody specific characteristics that empower them to continually seek to go beyond what they currently know. This disposition includes characteristics such as risk-taking, intellectual curiosity, persistence, and taking responsibility for one's decisions.

Recent examples of leadership, whether in government, corporations, media, and even the church, have emphasized style over substance, charisma over character, and self-centeredness over sacrificial service. As a result, people have become increasingly cynical, creating a loss of trust in leadership and organizations. The danger is that any significant change requires dynamic leaders to help people navigate previously uncharted terrain.

One of the most overused phrases of 2020 was "we are living in unprecedented times." However, just because a phrase is overused doesn't make it untrue. At least during our lifetimes, we had not experienced the combination of crises the year 2020 brought. Living and leading through a tri-demic—a health pandemic, a national financial crisis, and social unrest—presented corporate, political, and especially church leaders with enormous challenges, yet also some amazing opportunities.

The events of 2020 did not create the seismic changes the church and other entities had to address, but they dramatically accelerated the change. Ours was already becoming a digitally dominated culture. We were already dealing with increased autonomy and less dependence on hierarchal institutions. COVID-19 and the resultant social distancing measures served to force us to confront these realities much sooner than anyone had anticipated.

Analogous to how the novel coronavirus had greater adverse implications for those who had preexisting underlying health conditions, so did the rapid cultural shifts impact negatively churches that had preexisting, underlying spiritual and organizational conditions. Leadership that is incapable or unwilling to recognize the changing cultural landscape, learn from it, and change its response will experience greater dis-ease and more rapid decline.

Transformational leaders are keen students of contemporary culture while cultivating strong, deep roots in our spiritual and cultural heritage. They intentionally and continually refocus on their purpose, reviewing their practices, retooling their people, and striving to reach their potential.

If it is true, as Phyllis Tickle suggests, that "every five hundred years, the church cleans out its attic," then our work in this new season is to prayerfully discern those elements of our liturgies, polity, and practices that must be retained, retrieved, recycled, retooled, rejected, or respectfully retired. It is incumbent upon mature leaders to reflect carefully on those things that are integral to our mission and not recklessly discard priceless practices simply because they are a part of our tradition. However, for the church to "serve this present age" and beyond, we are challenged to intentionally scrutinize everything we do to ensure that we are movement crusaders, rather than museum curators.

Dr. J. Elvin Sadler profoundly articulates the imperative facing leaders to embrace change without rejecting the valuable treasures from our past that give us meaning and definition. The wonderful illustration he offers about changing the pot also reminds us of the importance of passing along our stories throughout the ages. Our ancestors may not get a veto over our choices, but they must be given a voice.

Bishop W. Darin Moore
Presiding bishop of the Mid-Atlantic Episcopal District
of The AME Zion Church and immediate past chair of the
National Council of Churches, USA

Preface

*I*f there ever was a need for transformative leadership, it is now. Yet it is absent from many organizations because the skills needed for such leadership are a unique combination of both art and science, relational and technical, interpersonal and corporate, poetry and prose, etc.

Across my span of thirty years in Charlotte, North Carolina, I have had the privilege of observing, both from a distance and up close, Dr. J. Elvin Sadler develop and thrive as a transformative leader. In a variety of settings, I've seen him positively alter the course of institutions and organizations with varying degrees of complexity.

In this work, *PotChangers: Innovative Change in an Ever-Changing World,* he shows us how. Utilizing the best of biblical insight, organizational development, and wisdom and wit from our elders, Dr. Sadler provides a playbook for transformation that can be applied to any group or system.

It is my prayer that as you read it, you will be blessed to grow in transformational agency.

Bishop Claude R. Alexander Jr.
Senior pastor
The Park Church
Charlotte, North Carolina

The Season of Unprecedented Rapid Change

I have been working on this book for quite some time. I would pick it up and put it down. I was never quite motivated to complete it until the "pandemic" hit. Then, there was an urgent drive for me to bring it to completion.

Pandemics, plagues, natural disasters, and economic collapses have caused us to change how we process and move information. Social networking, telepresence, video conferencing, email communication, and digital collaboration have shifted us into a culture that is changing at rapid speeds. Organizations that recognize rapid change and integrate innovative processes into their change culture will be those organizations that can use integrity, relationships, and trust to create cultures of innovative, lasting change.

As we move further into the twenty-first century, we must understand that adaptation and change are inevitable.

Innovative change processes are needed—desperately so—in this season.

As we move further into the twenty-first century, we must understand that adaptation and change are inevitable. How organizations and their leaders respond to these changes will help determine the existence and success of organizations or their failure and demise.

In this book, I draw upon more than forty years of experience as a pastor, judicatory leader, church thought leader, seminary mentor, and doctoral administrator to help you, the reader, discover how employing skill sets, resources, interpersonal characteristics, and organizational dynamics can help you become an effective, innovative change leader. The book covers a number of topics, ranging from the inevitability of change; the definition, archetypes, and characteristics of a PotChanger; the spirit of adventure; the critical necessity of trust; lessons learned from my mother; and the necessity of prayer. Also included is a real-life case study, which will show you how innovative change can help organizations navigate the fluctuating nuances they face in today's culture. Whether you are a young pastor navigating the waters of church culture, a seasoned pastor looking for ways to retool your current church model, or an experienced business leader looking for ways to reignite the vision of your organization, this book is for you!

Introduction

"It's Time to Change the Pot!"

A story is told about a young girl standing in the kitchen, watching as her mother cooked the family reunion dinner. It was a grand occasion, as four generations of the family gathered for this time of reflection and fellowship. The mother took out the family recipe for their favorite pot roast. This menu had been passed down from one generation to the next. The daughter watched eagerly as the mother seasoned the pot roast with all the familiar ingredients. Finally, the mother took the roast, cut off the ends, and placed it in the famous family pot. Curious about her mother's actions, the young girl asked her mother: "Mom, why did you cut off the ends of the roast before you placed it in the pot?"

The mother responded by saying, "Sweetie, I do not know. It's a family tradition. I saw your grandmother do it, and I'm just following her actions. Go and ask your grandmother why she cut the ends off the pot roast before placing it in the pot."

The young girl hurried into the next room. She asked her grandmother, "Granny, why do you cut off the ends of the pot roast before placing it in the pot?"

The grandmother responded by saying, "Baby, I do not know. I saw your great-grandmother cut the ends off the roast when I was a girl, and I just followed her actions. It's a family tradition. Go and ask your great-grandmother why she cuts the ends off the pot roast before she places it in the pot."

Eager to know, the young girl went over to her great-grandmother and asked, "Granny Grand, why did you cut off the ends of the pot roast before you placed it in the pot to cook?"

Sitting in her rocking chair and looking down over the rims of her glasses, the great-grandmother responded to her great-granddaughter by saying, "Well, baby, you see, the pot that I had wasn't big enough to hold the roast, so to make it fit, I had to cut off the ends to get it all in the pot."

What's the moral of this story? Always make sure you ask *why*. Generational inquiry necessitated the need to ask a question and ultimately to make an innovative change. Because the great-granddaughter asked the obvious question regarding an antiquated process (the use of a smaller pot), a need was discovered, and a strategy was changed (the use of a bigger pot) for greater effectiveness. Now the family will not have to cut up the roast, but, instead, they can just change the pot.

This story leads to a more pressing question: How many times do we continue to use outdated methods, whether in our homes, businesses, organizations, or houses of worship, without understanding that all we need to do is change the pot? How often do we continue to do something that we know doesn't make sense without asking why? This book will address an area of leadership that often brings an enormous amount of consternation and conflict: how to initiate and manage change in existing cultures to enlighten instead of to destroy organizations. While change is often necessary, and most times essential, to bring about ingenuity and innovation, many organizations fall short of effectively managing the process of integrating innovative change because they do not know how to facilitate the process and explain why the facilitation is critical to the ongoing vibrancy and life of an organization. I have discovered over my more than forty years of corporate and institutional experience, dealing with houses of worship, corporations, and leaders from around the world, that once leaders understand the significance of integrating innovative change into the culture of their organizations, not only do their organizations function more effectively, but they do so with a greater sense of purpose and intentionality.

The year 2020 has made this practice even more relevant. Even though we live in a continually evolving culture in which change is everywhere, no one knew, entering this year, that we would be confronted with a pandemic that would bring the world to a pause. Almost immediately, a global corporate, governmental, educational, and faith-centered community had to make innovative changes to deal with the ever-changing climate and culture caused by COVID-19. And it's not over; we are still living in this new reality. Those organizations that lay hold of these concepts and practices will enable their people to adapt and make the innovative changes necessary to be relevant, both in this year and in the years ahead. I hope that by the conclusion of reading this book, you will have a better understanding not only of why you need to facilitate innovative change, but also of how you can do so. And maybe, just maybe, you'll take the time to change the pot.

Chapter One

The Need to Change the Pot

"Progress is impossible without change, and those who cannot change their minds cannot change anything."

—George Bernard Shaw

The Inevitability of Change

The above quote by George Bernard Shaw holds an eternal truth: Progress is impossible without change. Every day, each of us are exposed to the nuances of change. One day ends with the sun setting, as another day births the sunrise of new possibilities. Seasons change as we shift from one to another. Fall's dropping of the trees' leaves ushers in winter's hibernating temperatures, which transition into the joyful springing of new life that takes its full shape in the warmth of summer.

There is an eternal truth here, which reinforces the reality that change is inevitable for humans. We experience an infant, in his or her total dependence on parental supervision and care, transition into the curiosity of a toddler, who transitions into a socially conscious and developmentally evolving child, who transitions into an independence-seeking, yet often-identity-confused adolescent, who ultimately becomes an adult: None of these would have been possible without change. The global onslaught of unavoidable change due to the rapidly evolving external factors of a worldwide pandemic has caused everyone to be exposed to a new understanding of systemic cultural fluidity. The Bible, in Romans 12:1–2, tells of the inevitable necessity of change in the renewing (changing) of one's mind: "I urge you, brothers and sisters, by the mercies of God, to present your bodies as a living and holy sacrifice, acceptable to God, which is your spiritual service of worship. And do not be conformed to this world, but be transformed [changed] by the *renewing* of your mind, so that you may prove what the will of God is, that which is good and acceptable and perfect" (emphasis mine). The bottom line is this: Regardless of the source, change is inevitable.

The Difficulty of Change

Even though we know that change is inevitable, most people have a hard time changing or accepting change in their lives. While there are various reasons people reject change, I believe that the driving force behind the rejection of change is fear.

Fear of the Unknown

One acronym for fear that gives us a better understanding of why people are so afraid is this: **F**alse **E**vidence **A**ppearing **R**eal. The driving factor for some is the fear of not knowing. People have various reasons for struggling with fear. Fear can arise for several reasons, such as not being informed of pertinent information, developing preconceived notions based upon others' experiences, or receiving inaccurate information based on false assumptions. Fear of the unknown can paralyze a person to the extent that he or she will not consider the notion of change.

Fear of Rejection

Another side effect of fear is rejection. Whether it's the rejection of an idea, a habit, a tradition, or a relationship, no one likes the feeling of being turned down. Often, the fear of rejection surfaces from past experiences of rejection. Once these past feelings surface, they can serve as a barrier to initiating change if left unchecked.

Fear of Exclusion

Exclusion is the act of denying a person access to or barring someone from a place, a group, or a privilege. Another word for *exclusion* is *alienation*. Humans are social beings. For the most part, we yearn to belong to something that connects us to a collective purpose or a goal greater or higher than anything we could experience by ourselves. When the possibility of change occurs, we fear the potential of being alienated, left out, or excluded because of changes to a system, organization, or process that may have included us and brought significance to our very existence as a part of the previous plan. Because of fear of the unknown, the threat or fear of alienation may cause a person to resist the possibility of change.

Fear of Being Obsolete

Just as there is nothing more powerful than an idea whose time has come, there is no greater feeling of inadequacy than to be a part of an idea that has run its course. To be obsolete means to be out-of-date, to be no longer able to produce or be used. The fear of obsolescence is the fear that once a person's usefulness is depleted, he or she no longer has any use or purpose. This phenomenon creates one of the most significant types of fear: *fear that I'm no longer needed.*

The Paralysis of Fear

All of these aspects of fear lead to a form of paralysis. People would prefer to shuffle around in a state of nonproductivity due to the fears of the unknown, rejection, exclusion, and obsolescence than to explore the enormous possibilities resulting from the change. The irony of this difficulty is that the very change that could catapult them into another season of productivity and relevance is the same change that causes them to be still and do nothing. When these fears are abated, and people are empowered to bring existing ideas and innovate them with fresh new perspectives, they discover that they can find their place of significance and contribute to the process of innovative change.

The Power of Innovative Change

While the fear of change can often be debilitating and subsequently paralyzing, we must begin to understand that: 1) change is necessary, and 2) there is an effective process, which, if implemented correctly, can help to alleviate the fears that are often associated with change. This process is called ***innovative change***. Innovative change is taking a ***principled tradition*** and enhancing it by merging an existing method with a newer, more effective approach to make the tradition more relevant and useful for the ***present*** culture and setting in which it currently exists. For us to more fully understand this process, we must understand principled traditions. A principled tradition is a well-established and fundamental process, system, rite, or act that has stood the test of time. In the introductory story regarding the pot, an innovative change occurred when the granddaughter made a generational inquiry: She asked, "why?" This generational inquiry was made to address the perceived need in the current generational setting to change the process of cooking the pot roast (a principled tradition). While there was nothing wrong with the recipe (a principled tradition) for the pot roast, the granddaughter perceived a better way to cook the pot roast. She didn't throw away the recipe (a principled tradition) that had been handed down over generations. She just felt there was a "better way" to cook the roast (to fulfill the principled tradition). Her ***generational inquiry*** (asking the right question to meet a specific need) brought about the clarity of purpose. It necessitated an innovative change in cooking the pot roast (a process of implementation).

The same holds true in much of life. While it may be the recipe for a pot roast in this scenario, there are numerous examples in which innovative change can radically affect how "business" is done. Whether in business, in government, or in faith, we have seen countless examples of outdated processes stifling the potential of a "principled tradition" continuing to be relevant and practical, all because the process of implementation was never updated.

Principled Traditions: Where Would We Be?

Innovative change has occurred throughout history. Where would we be today without innovative change? Where would we be if the Ford Motor Company continued to manufacture cars the way Henry Ford did with the Model T? Where would we be today if Apple continued to make computers as Steve Jobs did with the first Macintosh? If *Sports Illustrated* had understood that they were in the sports information and entertainment business rather than the magazine production business, there might never have been a need for ESPN. History has shown us that those organizations that have understood their purposes and principled traditions, and did not confuse them with the processes needed to make the principled traditions more effective, have been the ones to use innovative change to remain relevant and enhance the traditions that made them who they are today.

Throwing the Pot Roast Out with the Pot

What's the moral of this story? Do not throw out the proverbial pot roast with the pot. One of the biggest mistakes often made in facilitating change in business, government, and faith organizations is that leaders all too often want to throw everything out and begin anew. They want to throw the proverbial baby out with the bathwater, or, in this case, the pot roast out with the pot. While it is sometimes necessary to scrap a plan or process and completely develop a new one, most of the time this is not the case. The main reason people want to discard old systems and methods is that it takes time to bring about innovative change. However, I believe that many great ideas and dreams have been tossed out simply because leaders didn't take the time to involve themselves and their followers in the process of innovative change. While it may seem much easier to scrap a strategy and begin again, much can be lost in the process.

- **Effective systems may need to be changed**: Systems that have worked effectively in the past may need tweaking or retooling to become useful again.
- **Tried-and-true (*principled*) traditions can be lost**: While some traditions may have lost their relevance, many intergenerational traditions have stood the test beyond any specific timeframe.
- **Established relationships can be lost**: One of the dangers of participating in wholesale change is the risk of losing stakeholders who once bought in to the previous vision but now feel alienated because they have not been engaged in the new envisioning process.
- **The spirit of creativity can be lost**: When people feel that their opinions do not matter and the ideas of others are being forced upon them, they lose the desire to bring creativity to a new process.

Therefore, the PotChanger—the agent of change—must be sensitive to previous cultural dynamics and then strategically navigate and innovate necessary change without totally dismantling or eliminating a previous process unless it holistically is no longer relevant or of use to the success of the organization.

Dealing with Defective Pots

One might ask the question: Is there a need for PotChangers? The answer to this question is yes. For too long, many leaders have attempted to initiate change within their settings, only to find themselves either stifled by outdated methods that failed to bring the innovative process along in a way that created organizational synergy, or operating with "Lone Ranger" attitudes that ultimately resulted in corporate alienation and eventual burnout. Much of the dysfunction occurred as a result of dealing with dysfunctional leaders who displayed traits that were flawed in their approach to usher in and foster innovative change, such as:

Frail Pots

Frail pots consist of those leaders who have weathered the storms and been relatively successful in their endeavors. There is nothing wrong with the leader, except that age has inhibited the leader's ability to muster the energy to engage others in ongoing innovative change. While they are frail and may not have the physical strength to keep pace with an ever-changing marketplace, their wisdom and knowledge can be invaluable to those younger leaders who are willing to be mentored by them.

Irreparable Pots

Irreparable pots consist of those leaders who have been so severely damaged that it will take enormous amounts of therapy to rebuild trust and facilitate the process of innovative change. These people are often cynical about new ideas or methods and are resistant to change. They were raised in an era when they were "lorded over" by those in leadership. They prefer to remain with the status quo and frown upon those who might try to change it. The likelihood of these leaders being able to bring about sustainable, innovative change is improbable. The only prescription for those who fall into this category is the organizational emotional process, which we will turn to later.

Broken Pots

Broken pots are those leaders who had issues with their previous leaders, those who either lorded it over them in their approach to initiating change or disregarded them totally in their decision-making process. They became "yes men" who rubber-stamped their superiors and perpetuated the same model in their change process. While the likelihood of them being able to facilitate change is highly improbable, they can move toward becoming innovative agents of change with proper coaching.

Cracked Pots

Cracked pots are those leaders who can bring about innovative change but who have external issues that have hindered them in leading others through the process of change. Their issues typically stem from antiquated methods pulled from previously exposed models, and they never kept abreast of updated models for change. Because of this lack of exposure, they continued to engage the people in twentieth-century autocratic models while failing to realize that culture changes have necessitated a more relevant approach to participant engagement. The good news about the cracked pots is that although they were exposed to outdated practices, they are open to change and willing to make the necessary course corrections to foster innovative change.

Clay Pots

Clay pots are those leaders who have welcomed change throughout their entire careers. They have engaged others in collaborative consensus-building and are open to the ever-present notion of innovative change. They are called "clay pots" because they remain pliable and are not afraid to be molded and shaped into new and more creative forms of change. Their significance comes from their willingness to bring others along with them in the process. Because they understand the power of mentoring and are not afraid to share their wisdom with others, they create a legacy by shaping future generational leaders. These are the real PotChangers.

We have explored the various descriptions of different kinds of leaders. While each type can play an important role in how change occurs within their setting, not all of them were equipped to handle the way change must occur in the twenty-first century. We need innovative agents of change who are strong enough in their resolve and in their inner selves to honor and preserve the tenets that matter, while being flexible enough to bring about change as the need arises. The next chapter expounds on the characteristics of effective PotChangers.

Chapter Two

Effective PotChangers

"The two most important days in a person's life are the day they were born and the day they find out why."

—Mark Twain

What Should an Ideal Pot Look Like?

Identification and purpose are critical in the life of an innovative agent of change, or a PotChanger. If a person does not fully understand who they are or their nature, it will become challenging for them to lead others in anything of significance. Therefore, an individual must know, understand, and have confidence in their own abilities and limitations to effectively lead others in the process of innovative change. Now that we have become more acquainted with the various leadership styles, we must now look at the essential characteristics of effective PotChangers.

An effective PotChanger always makes sure that:

The Pot Is Clean

Another word for *clean* in this analogy would be the word *integrity.* One of the essential components to building an innovative change organization is building an organization of trust. In his groundbreaking work *The Speed of Trust,* Stephen Covey states:

> *There is one thing that is common to every individual, relationship, team, family, organization, nation, economy, and civilization throughout the world—one thing which, if removed, will destroy the most powerful government, the most successful business, the most thriving economy, the most influential leaders, the greatest friendship, the strongest character, the deepest love. On the other hand, if developed and leveraged, that one thing has the potential to create unparalleled success and prosperity in every dimension of life. Yet, it is the least understood, most neglected, and most underestimated possibility of our time. That one thing is* ***trust.***[1]

---

1 Stephen M.R. Covey, *The Speed of Trust: The One Thing That Changes Everything* (New York: Free Press, 2006), vii.

Trust is the foundational hallmark of establishing integrity. If an organization does not have trust in its leadership, the potential for facilitating necessary innovative change becomes quite limited. The importance of leaders keeping their word and following through with their stated goals and objectives is critical to move an organization through the change process.

The Pot Has No Leaks

In addition to a PotChanger having integrity, the leader must also establish a culture of trustworthiness. One of the most significant deterrents to lasting change and growth in a corporate environment occurs when an organization does not foster and encourage an atmosphere of trust. People are less inclined to contribute ideas when they feel they cannot trust the organization to credit their contributions. Fear of retribution for openness and honesty will cause employees not to share their true feelings on projects or processes if they feel they will be penalized for their candid remarks. People are afraid to explore and test new ways of doing things when they think that someone is always looking over their shoulder. Suppose organizations are going to experience real innovative change. In that case, they must make sure those in the organization feel safe to be open, creative, and candid in sharing ideas and recommendations that will benefit the organization for years to come.

The Pot Is Sufficient Enough to Handle the Ingredients

The PotChanger must also have the ability to create capacity for the organization. *Capacity* is the ability of an object to expand to the extent necessary to hold the contents it supports. An organization must be able to handle every aspect of its business in order for it to ensure it can perform at its optimal capacity. You might ask why this is so important. It is essential, because an organization that has not sufficiently handled and managed the people, products, resources, processes, and systems it has used in the past will have difficulty proving that it can effectively move through innovative change when it hasn't managed the previous structures of the organization. There is great wisdom in "making haste slowly." When an organization is deliberate in building its business model and makes concessions for growth, the organization will be more readily prepared to handle future changes and growth opportunities as they occur.

A PotChanger must have the skill sets and abilities necessary to develop a spirit of ***mutual collaboration*** *both within and outside of an organization.*

The Pot Is Flexible Enough to Complement Other Pots

A PotChanger must have the skill sets and abilities necessary to develop a spirit of *mutual collaboration* both within and outside of an organization. Collaboration is the ability to work well together with peers within an organization and with colleagues across organizations. Mutual collaboration is the leader's ability to work with other parties or organizations and provide assistance and support to others, whereby the interaction is mutually beneficial to all of the parties involved. Mutual collaboration is critical in the culture of specialization in which we live. Organizations are finding their niches in the marketplace by providing specialized services to their customers and constituents. When a need arises that is not handled by an organization but essential to their client base, the leader must find ways to collaborate with other organizations to cover the wide range of problems a customer may have at any given time. PotChangers who are sensitive to meeting their customers' needs will pursue relationships with colleagues across the business and faith spectrum to meet those needs.

The Pot Knows When It's Time to Change to Another Pot

A PotChanger must know when it is time to retool or retire and know the signs that will determine each. To know this, a PotChanger must have a clear sense of purpose and destiny. In the Old Testament, the prophet wrote in Jeremiah 29:11: "'For I know the plans that I have for you,' declares the Lord, 'plans for prosperity and not for disaster, to give you a future and a hope.'" Jeremiah's God told him there was both a plan and a purpose for the lives of Jeremiah and the children of Israel. A good leader will understand and become intimately acquainted with both his Creator and his moral compass. The two together will assist a PotChanger in knowing how and when to map out his or her journey. One of the greatest tragedies I've witnessed over the years are men and women who did not know the difference between retooling and retirement. I have seen many who have had excellent skill sets but who did not take the time to retool their talents to bring greater relevance and impact to their trades. And I've also seen those who had made great contributions to their fields of work, yet they did not know when it was time to retire. However, leaders who know and understand both their purpose in life and the destination where they are to arrive will be better equipped to make the necessary transitions at the appropriate times. An excellent example of knowing when to retool or retire is the decision made by Pope Benedict XVI of the Roman Catholic Church, the only pope to resign in the last six hundred years. When he was elevated to the papacy, he entered it with an express purpose and destiny. He knew what his role and timing were in the transition from Pope Saint John Paul II, to himself, to the elevation of Pope Francis in a time when the Roman Catholic Church faced "sexual abuse scandals" and "Vatican power struggles" that could have dismantled the entire institution.

Papal press spokesman Father Federico Lombardi stated this regarding his resignation:

> *The Church needed someone with more physical and spiritual energy who would be able to overcome the problems and challenges of governing the church in this ever-changing modern world. (BBC Radio, 28 November 2013)*[2]

Pope Benedict himself stated:

> *After having repeatedly examined my conscience before God, I have come to the certainty that my strengths, due to an advanced age, are no longer suited to an adequate exercise of the Petrine ministry.... In today's world, subject to so many rapid changes and shaken by questions of deep relevance for the life of faith, in order to govern the barque of Saint Peter and proclaim the Gospel, both strength of mind and body are necessary, strength which in the last few months, has deteriorated in me to the extent that I have had to recognize my incapacity to adequately fulfill the ministry entrusted to me. (Resignation statement, 11 February 2013)*[3]

---

2 See https://www.bbc.com/news/world-europe-21430737#:~:text=A%20day%20after%20Pope%20Benedict,because%20of%20any%20specific%20illness.

3 See https://www.reuters.com/article/us-pope-resigns-text/pope-resignation-announcement-text-idUSBRE91A0BS20130211.

Pope Benedict continues to live and be very impactful even in his retirement, as he recently celebrated more than sixty-five years in the priesthood at the time of this writing. He knew the difference between the time to retool and the time to retire.

Function and Purpose

Not only did Pope Benedict have an understanding of the difference between retooling and retirement, but he also understood the difference between ***function*** and ***purpose***. **Function** is the process by which we use our gifts, talents, and abilities, combined with our learned and innate competence and the skills we have to fulfill a task or assignment. It includes the completion of an assignment based upon a position or an office. When the assignment is completed for that particular position or office, we are then called to fulfill another assignment until all assignments have been fulfilled. **Purpose** involves the aggregation of all assignments, offices, and positions performed over a person's lifetime. It is the act of taking all of one's gifts, talents, and abilities, combining them with one's learned and innate competencies and skills, and merging them with one's career assignments and life experiences. All of them working together will identify the destiny that has been placed on one's life. The mapping of the events of a person's life helps to chart the course of the person's destiny or purpose. People often get the two confused. ***While function deals with fulfilling an assignment, purpose deals with fulfilling one's lifelong destination.*** For instance, consider a woman who graduates from college and takes a job as a corporate salesperson. The woman has the gifts of administration, teaching, and discernment, along with her learned and innate competencies. While she worked in corporate America, she used her talents and gifts to perform functions that made her successful as a sales manager by leading, training, and organizing her sales team. She was then called into the pastoral ministry. She used the same talents, gifts, and competencies to successfully train leaders and organize the church's various ministries while leading the church in growth and discipleship. Upon retirement from the pastoral ministry, she became a seminary professor, and eventually the seminary dean. She used the same administrative, teaching, and discerning gifts and her learned and innate competencies to successfully lead the seminary. Her assignments changed, but her talents, gifts, and learned and inherent skills and competencies remained the same. Her functions changed, but her purpose didn't; whether she was in the corporate, church, or seminary environment, her overall purpose was to equip leaders.

The problem that surfaces, for many leaders, is that they confuse function with purpose. They get stuck in an assignment because they make the assignment their purpose, when all the assignment was meant to be was a function of their purpose. *But when leaders begin to understand their overall purpose, they can fulfill it in whatever environment they find themselves.* And that is only half of it. Legacy is built when leaders who understand how to find their purpose serve as mentors to help others identify their purpose! It's what the apostles of Jesus did in Acts chapter six. They understood that their purpose was not to wait on tables; it was to attend to prayer and the ministry of the Word to lead God's people. Finding purpose is what God has called each of us, as leaders, to do.

The late Dr. Miles Munroe, in his book *In Pursuit of Purpose,* said it like this: "When our purpose in life has been fulfilled, God takes us home."[4] In the New Testament, Jesus says it like this: "Well done, good and faithful slave. You were faithful with a few things, I put you in charge of many things; enter the joy of your master" (Matthew 25:23). While the assignment you're in now may be a worthy profession, it may not be your final destination. Seek God's purpose for your life and watch Him chart a clear pathway to your destiny!

---

4 Myles Munroe, *In Pursuit of Purpose* (Shippensburg, PA: Destiny Image, 1991).

Chapter Three

Biblical Examples of a PotChanger

There are many examples of biblical leaders who possessed innovative change characteristics, such as Joseph, Moses, Joshua, David, Hezekiah, Solomon, and the like. They all had qualities essential to create communities of innovative change. In this chapter, we will focus on biblical leaders who possessed the characteristics of effective PotChangers.

I. Elijah: Totally Relied on the Power of God to Lead Him in All Situations

Spiritual Integrity

> *Then at the time of the offering of the evening sacrifice, Elijah the prophet approached and said, "LORD, God of Abraham, Isaac and Israel, today let it be known that You are God in*

> *Israel and that I am Your servant, and that I have done all these things at Your word. Answer me, LORD, answer me, so that this people may know that You, LORD, are God, and that You have turned their heart back." Then the fire of the LORD fell and consumed the burnt offering and the wood, and the stones and the dust; and it licked up the water that was in the trench. When all the people saw this, they fell on their faces; and they said, "The LORD, He is God; the LORD, He is God!"*
>
> —1 Kings 18:36–39

One of the greatest tools a leader must have if they are to lead those who follow them through innovative change is a direct connection to a Source greater than themselves. Elijah connected to the Source of all that made Elijah who he was: Israel's sovereign God, Elohim. Because of his relationship to his God and reliance upon the power of God, Elijah was able to totally rely upon the power of God to lead him in all situations. Elijah did this by adhering to the following two principles:

1. Elijah Didn't Move until He Heard from God.

The secret to Elijah's success was his obedience in not moving until God gave him direction. Whenever Elijah was confronted with any situation, whether it involved God bringing drought and subsequent famine, the raising of a widow's son from death, or the display of God's power to diminish the authority of foreign gods, Elijah didn't move until he was led to move by God. As Elijah totally relied upon the direction of God, so must PotChangers. Leaders often make the mistake of following their own direction rather than seeking divine guidance (inner self-direction through the power of the Word and the Spirit) to make decisions that will bring about innovative change. Because there is no "higher power" that helps them set their moral compass, they rely upon circumstances and situations, which can often become blurred or skewed by external forces. PotChangers must have an internal guide that leads them properly, regardless of the external forces around them.

2. Elijah Exhibited a Boldness Based upon Prior Experiences.

One of the greatest attributes of mastering innovative change is the experience that comes along with it. Experiencing innovative change fosters boldness to face future possibilities of change as they occur. One of the greatest attributes Elijah had was the experience of being able to depend on God. Although Elijah experienced his run-ins with Jezebel, one thing he knew he could depend on was the power and presence of God available whenever Elijah needed Him. And whenever Elijah heard from God and followed the plan of God, Elijah experienced the success of God. PotChangers must realize that in order to be successful, they must know

An innovative agent of change must possess the ability to accurately discern the point of view of a particular situation from an elevated position.

when to implement change and then have the boldness to do it without delay. They must be willing to operate with boldness, based upon prior experiences.

Because of Elijah's willingness to yield to the all-sufficient power of God and allow God to be his Source and Guide in all his endeavors, he was not only able to be successful, but he also left a foundation to build for Elisha, who succeeded him.

II. Jesus: Had a Keen Perspective and Core Values That Continually Kept Him Grounded

Cultural and Internal Sensitivity

Filippo Brunelleschi was a fifteenth-century Italian architect who was considered to be a founding father of Renaissance architecture. He was a designer and is now recognized as the first modern engineer, planner, and sole construction supervisor. He is most famous for designing the dome of the Florence Cathedral, a feat of engineering that had not been accomplished since antiquity.[5] In circa 1420, after spending

[5] See https://en.wikipedia.org/wiki/Filippo_Brunelleschi.

five years developing a theory, he proved the mathematical technique called linear perspective. *Linear perspective* is the "art of representing three-dimensional objects on a two-dimensional surface to give the right impression of their height, width, depth, and position in relation to each other."[6] It is a type of mathematical equation used by artists in which the relative size, shape, and position of objects are determined by drawn or imagined lines converging at a point on the horizon. Perspective helps to give the viewer a scaled version that resembles how something will look in reality. One of the most important attributes an innovative agent of change must possess is the ability to accurately discern the point of view of a particular situation from an elevated position: The higher the elevation, the greater and more precise the view, and ultimately a more accurate global perspective. They must have a proper perspective on the situation. Jesus' perspective was different from all others in the earth because He viewed humanity from a totally different elevation. Because His Kingdom was not of this world, He approached every situation from a heavenly point of view. As PotChangers, leaders must have a proper perspective of their setting and culture, relative and in relation to other settings and cultures around them. This is so important because leaders are faced with making difficult decisions daily. From decisions regarding

[6] See https://www.lexico.com/en/definition/perspective.

vision, promotion, staffing, employment, policies and procedures, and corporate goodwill and community impact to product/ministry development and product or ministry placement and procurement, a PotChanger needs to know when to act or remain still, to maintain the present course or to change it altogether. Many of these decisions will impact generations yet unborn.

Position and Discernment

Two variables that are critical to a leader having a proper perspective are position and discernment. ***Position*** is the place from which a leader sits or stands to gain perspective. The higher the elevation, the greater the ability to see the situation more globally; the closer in proximity to a setting to view the situation, the better the understanding of the situation. Both height and proximity are crucial to gaining a proper perspective.

One of the dangers of improper positioning is gaining a false sense of perspective. I warn leaders all the time to be careful about how they judge another person's perspective. Be careful of placing yourself in another person's shoes if you haven't measured their shoe size and walked in similar shoes. Unless and until you are in a position of elevation to view the situation globally and close enough in proximity to examine the situation more specifically, you should not rush to judgment on how a matter should be handled. One of the great amusements I have witnessed has been to see assistant ministers criticize and ridicule senior pastors about how they have handled a particular situation. They always have it all worked out in their minds; they say, "If I had been given the opportunity, I would have handled that situation differently," until they are given the opportunity to become a pastor themselves. They then realize all the intricacies and the burdens associated with pastoring a congregation of people. Their conversation changes because they have seen pastoring from a different point of view. My advice to all leaders is this: Be careful about making rash remarks regarding the decisions that others make about their setting. Even within their environment, they should be sure to carefully examine every situation before making any decision. I tell them to employ the principle of the snake.

The Principle of the Snake

In Matthew 10:16, Jesus makes this statement: "Behold, I send you out as sheep in the midst of wolves. Therefore be wise as serpents and harmless as doves" (NKJV). The word "serpent" is the Greek word *ophis*,[7] and it merely describes a snake of any type, but it is used here as a sign of cunningness or cleverness. Matthew 10:16 had always perplexed me because I had previously thought of a serpent as being only evil. But

7 See https://en.wiktionary.org/wiki/ophis.

as I meditated on this verse more deeply, I began to gain new insight into what Jesus was saying. He was saying that serpents are "wise," and we need to take a lesson from them!

If you're a little squeamish about the subject of serpents or snakes, stay with me for the next few moments so you do not miss the full impact of what Jesus was telling us. He is the One who chose to use a serpent to make His point!

Snakes, blend into the environment when they move into new territory.

What intrigued me in this passage is Jesus' notion of a "wise serpent." I live in the Piedmont region of North Carolina. It is known for its beautiful lakes and its warm and humid climate in the summer. It is also known for copperheads. During the summer, because of their cold-blooded nature, these snakes try to find cool places to dwell. I then began to study what a serpent, or a snake, does when it comes to a new environment. I believe if we follow these same principles as we seek to gain perspective, it will impact our ability to assess any situation accurately.

The snake slowly moves into a new environment, with as little fanfare as possible.

The one thing a snake does not want to do is to be seen while moving into a new environment. Being seen puts the snake in jeopardy of either being seen by prey or being discovered by predators. The snake, stealthily and without fanfare, makes its way into a new environment. Snakes, therefore, blend into the environment when they move into new territory. Rather than announce their presence, they lie low, stay quiet, and blend into their surroundings. You could walk right past a snake and not know you're close to it!

Most snakes have the ability to be nearly invisible when they enter a new environment. This camouflage serves as a protective "covering." Even the fiercest aggressor could pass by, but the serpent would not likely be noticed, because it blends so well into the landscape.

The season of camouflage is a time that allows the serpent to find its way around new territory. It will enable it to move about freely while "evaluating" a unique situation. Serpents will assess their surroundings to identify places of shelter so they can settle into a new environment. They find hiding places to protect themselves from attack. It is also a time for them to observe where to find the easiest prey. When all of these evaluations and facts are accumulated, the serpent is ready to act. This "settling in" period is a crucial time for the reptile.

The snake observes the land and looks for opportunities for both prey and predators.

The first thing a snake does is observe his environment. He does this for a couple of reasons: First, he does it to know what is available to provide him with a source of nourishment. If there are not opportunities for rodents or other food supplies present, this might not be the right place for habitation. But if the environment is suitable for "pickings," the snake prepares to take up residence.

Second, the snake observes the environment to search for threats to his existence. If there are open spaces where birds may swoop in and capture them or humans or other species that might trap them, then the environment might not be conducive for living. But if the risk for capture is less than the reward for prey, the snake will take up residence.

The snake determines the proper time to strike.

Once the snake has come into an environment and made all necessary observations of predator and prey, the right opportunity presents itself, and the snake strikes. The snake's ultimate goal is to strike to eat, grow, and survive within an environment without running the risk of placing its life in jeopardy.

The same is true for an innovative leader. If a leader does not have a clear perspective on setting and culture, they may risk making decisions that will adversely impact those around them. As it would become disastrous for a naval officer to miscalculate the missile coordinates to destroy an enemy vessel and, instead, destroy a neighboring village, the same would hold for a PotChanger who mistakenly determines the course an organization must take to ensure its future survival. An incorrect perspective could affect the direction and impact of the organization for years to come. The leader must take the time to assess the environment before effectively making any significant decisions. Leaders must do a **contextual analysis.**

Contextual Analysis

A contextual analysis is the act of analyzing one's setting of ministry or business. To understand what a contextual analysis is, we must first understand the definition of *setting*. The setting is the set of circumstances that form the setting for an event, statement, or idea in terms that can be fully understood and assessed. It is the act of investigating everything associated with the setting to make an accurate diagnosis and course of action to address the setting's issues. Performing a contextual analysis involves several vital components.

1. **Historical Analysis:** The pastor or leader, as a historian, must research the history of the setting. Understanding its founding and the founder(s), under

what circumstances it was founded, major events in the development of the ministry or business, and significant changes in the ministry's life will help give a better understanding of the current character of the enterprise.

2. **Demographical Analysis:** The agent of change must understand the demographical makeup of the setting. The leader must know the different generational groupings of the cultural setting. What age grouping makes up most of your setting? Is it a young, vibrant setting; a middle-aged or mature setting; or an aging, less-active setting? What is the socioeconomic status of the setting? Is the setting made up of blue-collar, middle-class, upper-middle-class, or wealthy persons? Does the setting have members of influence in society, or are the members more involved at the grassroots level? The leader must also assess the climate of the community in which the setting dwells. Is it rural, urban, or suburban? Is it thriving, stable, or declining, and what is the forecast for its foreseeable future?
3. **Congregational Setting:** The final area of analysis is on the personality and character of the congregation or ministry. What is the character of the ministry? Is the setting traditional or contemporary? Does change

happen readily, or is there a resistance to change? Do leaders honor the chief leader's decisions, or do they resist and fight those decisions? Is the setting family-centered or ministry-centered? Do tradition, maintenance, or ministry drive money decisions? Does the setting have a "pedestal" mentality, where all responsibility is placed upon the leader to do everything, or is there a shared ministry model, where leaders are empowered to execute ministry based upon spiritual gifts?

Once the leader has thoroughly analyzed all facets of the setting, a plan can be developed either to continue the setting's direction or make necessary innovative changes or course corrections to enhance the ministry's effectiveness. Some may ask, how long should it take to conduct an evaluative process? The answer is: as long as it takes to assess the situation thoroughly. For some, it may take a year to understand all the intricacies and nuances of the setting's culture. For others, it could take longer, depending on the extenuating circumstances of a church split or a leader's moral failure. Regardless of how long it takes, do the analysis correctly. Many leaders make hasty decisions about their setting and go in with the idea of changing everything to suit their needs and desires. This is a dangerous practice. Leaders who take the time to do the necessary work to evaluate and understand their setting adequately position themselves for a fruitful and productive ministry. Bottom line: *Take the time to get to know your setting.*

Core Values

One of the most important attributes an effective leader must possess that will help the leader maintain a proper perspective while remaining grounded is core values. A set of core values must govern innovative leaders. *Core values* is another term for guiding principles. Core values are guiding principles that help to chart the course for everything the leader says and does. These principles are nonnegotiable values that a leader uses to govern their life. One of the most significant examples of an innovative leader that ruled His life by a set of core values was Jesus. He not only had an internal compass that helped to chart His course (the Holy Spirit), but He also had a set of core values that governed everything He did; He called these core values the ***Beatitudes.*** **The Beatitudes were and are eternal principles that cause a person to be blessed or to live a blessed or prosperous life.** The Beatitudes consist of nine fundamental beliefs that Jesus espoused as the keys to creating and sustaining a life of significance.

In Matthew 5:1–16 (KJV), Jesus said this:

And seeing the multitudes, he went up into a mountain: and when he was set, his disciples came unto him: And he opened his mouth, and taught them, saying, "Blessed are the poor in spirit: for theirs is the kingdom of heaven. Blessed are they that mourn: for they shall be comforted. Blessed are the meek: for they shall inherit the earth. Blessed are they which do hunger and thirst after righteousness: for they shall be filled. Blessed are the merciful: for they shall obtain mercy. Blessed are the pure in heart: for they shall see God. Blessed are the peacemakers: for they shall be called the children of God. Blessed are they which are persecuted for righteousness' sake: for theirs is the kingdom of heaven. Blessed are ye, when men shall revile you, and persecute you, and shall say all manner of evil against you falsely, for my sake. Rejoice, and be exceeding glad: for great is your reward in heaven: for so persecuted they the prophets which were before you. Ye are the salt of the earth: but if the salt have lost his savour, wherewith shall it be salted? It is thenceforth good for nothing, but to be cast out, and to be trodden under foot of men. Ye are the light of the world. A city that is set on a hill cannot be hid. Neither do men light a candle, and put it under a bushel, but on a candlestick; and it giveth light unto all that are in the house. Let your light so shine before men, that they may see your good works, and glorify your Father which is in heaven."

The revelation and reality of the Beatitudes are that Jesus first shared the values that governed His life, and then, for the next three and a half years, He was intentional about modeling the behavior of these core values He had shared with the people.

He shared with them how to:

- **Be Poor in Spirit:** What does it mean to be poor in spirit? Does it mean that a person has become so impoverished that there is no spirit? No. It means that a person has become so aware of the depravity of their spirit that they yearn to be filled with God's Spirit. Jesus challenged the people to discover the depth of their spiritual depravity and to ask God to give them the wisdom and discernment they needed to allow Christ's Spirit to immerse them and overtake them fully.
- **Be Mournful:** To mourn deals with the godly sorrow a person displays due to the knowledge of their depravity of sin. When we are sorrowful, not only for our sins but also for the sins of the world, the result should lead us to repentance. It is in the place of repentance that we are restored to our place of fellowship with the Father. And it is the reconnection of fellowship with the Father that brings us comfort. Jesus challenged the people to ask God for

the discernment that made them aware of sin in and around their lives so they could turn from it and be reconciled to God.

- **Be Meek:** What does it mean to be meek? Is meekness the same as weakness? Absolutely not. Meekness is the act of exhibiting strength under control. It is the act of a person having every right to lash out at another but choosing instead to allow his or her response to be measured. Meekness is not an act of the natural self; it is enabled by the Holy Spirit's power and control. Jesus challenged the people to allow the Holy Spirit to assist them in measuring their responses to any situation that might cause them to act before they thought.
- **Hunger and Thirst after Righteousness:** What does it mean that those who hunger and thirst after righteousness will be filled? It means that those who have a desire to align their lives with the will of God and follow His precepts in everything they do will receive divine sustenance that satisfies their every need each day. Such people will want for nothing, because their wills will line up with the will of God. Jesus challenged the people to seek the will of God for their lives, to find those things that would bring them into divine alignment with Him. Jesus promised they

would experience the fullness of (be filled with) God's blessings in everything they did.

- **Be Merciful:** *Mercy* is defined as "compassion or forgiveness shown toward someone within one's power to punish or harm." What does it mean to be merciful (*eleēmōn*)? Is it the act of showing compassion toward others as a result of them showing kindness toward us? Absolutely not! To be merciful means to display empathy toward others even when it is in your right and power to punish or harm them. It is an earnest response to the compassion God shows toward us, even though we deserve otherwise. Jesus challenged the people to find ways to express God's lovingkindness toward those whom they thought didn't deserve it.
- **Be Pure in Heart:** What does it mean to be pure in heart? Does it mean that a person is removed from sin's grasp? No. It means that they are aware of the depravity of sin but have chosen to rid themselves of those things that would cause broken fellowship with the Father. To "see God" means to walk in such a way that no hindrance comes between you and your intimacy with Him; there is no broken fellowship. Jesus challenged the people to seek holiness, to

remove all distractions, and to find ways to live a life of unbroken fellowship with the Father.

- **Be a Peacemaker:** What does it mean to be a peacemaker? It means that our every action should be centered on seeking and keeping peace at all costs. Peacemakers seek to fulfill the ministry of reconciliation. The designation of "children of God" comes as a result of their desire to seek peace. Jesus challenged the people to seek out ways to promote peace in everything they said and did.
- **Be Persecuted for Righteousness' Sake:** What does it mean to be persecuted for righteousness' sake? Along with that question, what is righteousness? It is the act of living your life aligned with the will of God. To be persecuted for righteousness' sake means that you are persecuted for being in God's will. It is the act of being subjected to punishment for being in and honoring the will of God. Jesus taught the people not to be discouraged when others persecuted them for doing what was right. God will grant them access to the Kingdom for their obedience. Jesus challenged them to pursue righteousness at all costs: the greater the pursuit, the greater the alignment, and the greater the alignment, the greater the access.

- **Have Endurance:** What benefit is it of ours to be lied about, reviled, and persecuted for the sake of following Christ? While it may be uncomfortable and seem worthless, it is of great reward. Jesus said that when we go through these things for His sake, our response should be to rejoice because we are in good company; they did the same thing to the prophets. Jesus challenged them never to allow false accusations, persecution, or revilement to enter and cause them to forsake the truth.
- **Jesus then gave them the core values of being like salt and light.** Jesus taught them where, how, and when to pray, and where and how to give. He taught them the principle of focus and how not to be distracted by the things of the world. He taught them about the harmful and destructive effects of judging and the power of forgiveness, and He modeled it, even to the point of death. He let them know, above all else, that their aim should be to seek first the Kingdom of God and His righteousness, and that all the things they both needed and longed for would be added unto them (Matthew 6:33, author paraphrase).

Core values, effectively established, become the foundation that help PotChangers shape and maintain the trust.

Jesus lived and governed His life by a set of guiding principles that caused Him to never waver, even when facing the cruelest penalty for our sins: death on the cross. It was because of His unalterable belief in these guiding principles that He never faltered or failed. Core values, effectively established, become the foundation that help PotChangers shape and maintain the trust and integrity needed to bring about the necessary innovative change.

III. Sons of Issachar: Understood the signs of the times and always looked for cutting-edge ways to serve those in and beyond their settings

Global Discernment

> *"Culture, not vision or strategy, is the most powerful factor in any organization."*
>
> —Samuel R. Chand,
> *Cracking Your Church's Culture Code*

One of the most critical attributes a PotChanger should have is the ability to assess their culture and setting accurately. Culture consists of the beliefs, behaviors, objects, and other characteristics common to the members of a particular group or society. Setting consists of the circumstances that form the setting for an event or set of events, statements, or ideas in terms that can be fully understood and assessed. Culture consists of the intrinsic characteristics, those dynamics that affect a particular group or society's emotional, intellectual, and spiritual factors. It deals with the spirit or ethos of the group or organization. Setting deals with the external characteristics, those dynamics that affect history, demographics, and conditions of a group or society. It deals with the current environment of the group. As changes in the weather affect the dynamics of an environment, so do the changes in culture affect the setting's dynamics. A leader cannot effectively bring about innovative change without fully understanding the dynamics of both culture and setting. If a leader tries to implement change while only understanding culture and not fully interpreting and addressing the setting, the group's spirit may change. Still, the environment may remain the same or even worsen. Likewise, if the setting is addressed and the culture is ignored, there may be an external change of appearance but no internal lasting transformation. But when both are adequately analyzed, an innovative course of action can be prescribed to bring about contextual understanding and synergy and lasting cultural healing and transformation. There is no better biblical example of understanding the signs of the times, through culture and setting, than the sons of Issachar.

> *From the sons of Issachar, men who understood the times, with knowledge of what Israel should do....*
>
> —1 Chronicles 12:32

Not much is mentioned regarding the sons of Issachar. However, we know that Issachar was the ninth son of Jacob, born to Leah, who bought time from Rachel in order to be with Jacob. Issachar was therefore known as the man of hire. Jacob bestowed a prophetic blessing upon Issachar and stated that he would be compared to a strong donkey, both a beast of burden and one who had a wild side. The sons of Issachar were great manual laborers and the third largest of the tribes of Israel. The thing that made them so prosperous was that they had the uncanny ability to identify the land that would give them the best chance for success. Through astrology and physical science, they were able to effectively assess their territory and cultivate it for their maximum benefit. Even though their prosperity eventually caused their demise, due to foreign enemies robbing them of their environment because of its richness, they were able to assess a situation and work to make it the best it could be.

As innovative agents of change ourselves, there are several lessons we can take from the sons of Issachar:

1. **Do not despise what has been given to us.**

The sons of Issachar did not wallow in the fact that other tribes might have been given what they believed to be a better territory. They took what they had and used it to its fullest ability. Innovative leaders must approach their setting the same way. There is no perfect setting; everything comes with positives and negatives. The key to ushering in a spirit of transformative change is not despising the day of small beginnings. Take what has been given to you and make the best of it.

2. **Take what has already been given to us.**

God has already blessed us with distinctive gifts. Whether it be a newly appointed call to pastor a congregation, an existing business, an out-of-date vision, a complacent team, or an underperforming organization, take the time to discover the wealth of resources already deeply embedded in the soil of the setting, then cultivate the culture in such a way that will bring about renewed vitality.

3. **Use your abilities and hard work to bring about lasting, innovative, transformative change.**

The sons of Issachar used their skills in astrology and physical science, combined with their strong work ethic, to make their territory the best it could be. Use what you have. God has given it to you for a reason. Do not get stuck on looking at what others have. You are uniquely gifted for the task before you. And always remember that hard work pays off! Proverbs 26:15 (NIV) states: "A sluggard buries his hand in the dish; he is too lazy to bring it back to his mouth." Never underestimate the power of hard work; it will pay off.

Bringing about innovative change can be difficult. It may seem as if no progress is being made. The key is to understand your culture, take what's before you, and use the skills and resources available to bring about lasting transformative change.

IV. Barnabas: Always looked for other PotChangers and sought opportunities to fellowship and be in covenant with them.

Hospitable Engagement

> *Now Joseph, a Levite of Cyprian birth, who was also called Barnabas by the apostles (which translated means Son of Encouragement), owned a tract of land. So he sold it, and brought the money and laid it at the apostles' feet.*
>
> —Acts 4:36-37

Many great characters in the Bible helped to shape the story of God's love and plans of deliverance and salvation for humanity, such as Moses, Joshua, David, Solomon, Peter,

James, and John. There are also those characters who are recognized to have served significantly to impact the spreading of the Gospel of Christ. One such person was a man named Joseph. But we are not talking about Jesus' earthly father, Joseph, or the aristocratic leader Joseph of Arimathea. He requested the body of Jesus and allowed Jesus' body to be placed in his family's tomb. The Joseph we speak of today is of Cyprian birth, and he became an apostle. But Joseph is not known for his mighty acts or even the preaching of the gospel. Joseph is known for a character trait he displayed that helped make the execution of ministry more tolerable and achievable to those around him. Joseph is known as Barnabas. Barnabas was a Levite, a native of the island of Cyprus. He was an avid supporter of the Kingdom. He sacrificed his possessions (his land), sold it, and brought the profit and laid it at the apostles' feet. He was also known for his enormous generosity shown to Paul, financially supporting Paul's ministry.

But above all this, Barnabas is known for another unique and necessary gift. The apostles named him Barnabas because *Barnabas* means "son of encouragement" (see Acts 4:36). Barnabas spoke so much encouragement into the lives of all those around him that the title "son of encouragement" became his actual name. After Paul's conversion on the road to Damascus, Barnabas courageously vouched for him when the leaders in Jerusalem became suspicious that this former persecutor of the followers of Christ wanted to proclaim the gospel now. As a leader and preacher of the gospel, he was sent to minister to the church at Antioch. It is stated that:

> *When he [Barnabas] came and saw the grace of God, he was glad, and he exhorted them all to remain faithful to the Lord with steadfast purpose, for he was a good man, full of the Holy Spirit and of faith. And a great many people were added to the Lord.*
>
> —Acts 11:23–24 (ESV)

After he arrived in Antioch, Barnabas encouraged Paul to help him with the work. Together, they equipped and empowered leaders to preach God's Word and fulfill His ministry. Later, Barnabas and Paul accompanied one another on their first missionary journey, having heard from God during a season of fasting and praying.

Later, Barnabas and Paul had a sharp disagreement. This caused them to agree to depart from one another, mutually. This occurred because Barnabas wanted to take John Mark along on their missionary journey, while Paul did not want to because John Mark had abandoned them previously. Because of his spirit of encouragement, Barnabas stuck up for his cousin John Mark, and Paul chose Silas to travel with him.

Barnabas left a tremendous legacy. Barnabas's actions and ministry proved him to be a strong man of faith. He left a lasting legacy that will be remembered wherever the story of the early advancement of the Kingdom is preached. Encouragement is also essential in the life of an innovative leader. Because people are so reluctant to change and change is often an arduous and time-consuming process, a spirit of encouragement is critical in developing a changing culture. If innovative leaders are going to be successful in ushering in transition, they must create a culture of encouragement. Followers must be reminded of the purpose of change, and as milestones are met, they must be acknowledged and celebrated. When they are faced with opposition and confronted with naysayers, positive affirmations must be put in place to offset negative confessions. There may even come times when opposing opinions rise that jeopardize the change process. When these situations come, innovative leaders must make the difficult decision to differ with, or even part ways with, those who may oppose, for the sake of promoting the greater good. When encouragement is combined with the motivation to change, creating new and more relevant models for business and ministry effectiveness will leave a lasting impact that shapes culture for future innovative change. What an amazing legacy to leave behind when you are known as an innovative leader who poured encouragement and hope into the lives of those connected to you! Be a "son of encouragement"!

V. The apostle Paul: Sought opportunities to identify, nurture, and develop future PotChangers to continue a legacy of effective leadership succession.

Progenitorial Significance

> *I do not write these things to shame you, but as my beloved children I warn you. For though you might have ten thousand instructors in Christ, yet you do not have many fathers; for in Christ Jesus I have begotten you through the gospel. Therefore I urge you, imitate me. For this reason I have sent Timothy to you, who is my beloved and faithful son in the Lord, who will remind you of my ways in Christ, as I teach everywhere in every church.*
>
> —1 Corinthians 4:14-17 (NKJV)

One of the greatest dangers to the life and continued existence of any organization is the failure to develop a leadership succession plan. One thing in life is certain: All things must come to their intended end, including leaders. Whether you are a leader of a church, a not-for-profit organization, an institution of higher learning, or a corporation, finding, nurturing, and mentoring future leaders is the key to ensuring the successful future and transition of the organization from one leader and generation to another.

Leadership succession planning is essential for several reasons:

1. **It ensures a successful transition.**

There is not a more important element in the life of an organization than the element of positive momentum. Positive momentum is how an organization continues to build upon its successes, from one success to another. When an organization fosters an atmosphere of positive momentum, it in turn produces an attitude of corporate enthusiasm in every facet of its business environment. A key to maintaining positive momentum is having a detailed plan of succession in place. When an organization is aware that present leadership has taken the time to plan for the transition and succession of future leadership properly, it communicates to other members of the organization that time has been spent to ensure the organization continues to be successful.

2. **It reduces the stress of the unknown.**

One of the greatest hindrances to the morale of an organization is the fear of the unknown. I have discovered that while people may not like bad news, the process of waiting for the possibility of bad news can be even more damaging. It becomes more harmful because it gives people the opportunity and time to form their own imagined scenarios regarding a particular matter. This can be both damaging to the atmosphere of the organization and ultimately counterproductive to the ongoing momentum. Leaders must be sensitive to the adverse effects that arise from keeping organizational members in the dark. Members appreciate when an organization is both open and honest regarding succession and transition. While people may dread the thought of new leadership and the possibilities of what it might bring, they will appreciate openness and the organization's willingness to involve them in some measure of the transition.

3. **It fosters continuity of vision and mission.**

Nothing is more critical to creating a healthy organizational culture than a clear direction for its future. Clear vision and mission help foster this climate, and they foster it even more when members realize that there will be continuity of vision and mission with new leadership. An effective succession plan will promote continuity, because the new leadership can be immersed in the organizational culture's vision and mission. When this happens, there is a greater probability that the vision and mission will be built upon and strengthened rather than destroyed and thrown away. However, there will be times when the vision and mission have not fostered the positive growth expected. When this happens, new leadership is necessary to become aware of the areas of success and challenge to assess where change needs to occur effectively. In either scenario, proper succession planning will help to preserve and innovate what's successful and modify and change what is not.

4. It preserves a legacy.

Legacy is the act of preserving the history of a person or organization. It communicates to all involved the tenets and principles that were held to be sacred and transformative. Legacy is the bridge that connects one generation to the next. When an organization is intentional about preserving legacy during the transition, it says to those left behind that what has been done in the past is valued by those who will succeed in the future.

Biblical Leadership Succession

Leadership succession planning is not a twenty-first-century phenomenon; succession planning goes as far back as history records. More specifically, let's look at a snapshot of models of succession planning that took place in the Bible. Abraham, the father of faith, was succeeded by his son Isaac, who was succeeded by his son Jacob, who was succeeded by his eleventh son, Joseph, who became second-in-charge to the pharaoh of Egypt's nation. Moses, who led the children of Israel out of Egypt's bondage, was succeeded by Joshua, who ushered them into the Promised Land. Saul, who became Israel's first earthly king, was followed by David, who became Israel's greatest earthly king, and he was succeeded by his son Solomon. Elijah, with his prophetic mantle, spoke the Word of God with authority and performed many miracles and great signs; he was succeeded by his adjutant, Elisha, who received a double portion of Elijah's mantle. Jesus, who identified His disciples and nurtured them, chose from the seventy, twelve apostles who succeeded Him upon His ascension to His rightful place beside God the Father in heaven. And those apostles chose, from among them, men and women who would learn from them and ultimately carry the mantle of responsibility to lead the early church and win souls for Christ. The Bible is replete with succession models that reflect the wisdom of preparing others to assume the mantle of responsibility upon the completion of the present leader's assignment.

Let's look at an example of succession preparation and planning that has blessed the lives of people of the Christian faith for more than two thousand years: the apostle whose name was Paul.

The Conviction of Saul

Paul, who was born a pure Hebrew ("a Hebrew of Hebrews") from the tribe of Benjamin, the twelfth son of Jacob, an erudite scholar of Israel's law, as a Pharisee, and a citizen of Rome, is considered by many to be the greatest church planter that has ever lived. But before he became an apostle named Paul, he was known as the persecutor of the Christians named Saul. Saul was a devout Jew. He studied under the great Jewish rabbi and scholar Gamaliel. But he was infamously known as one of the greatest persecutors of the Christians. He led several assaults on Christians and murdered them for their faith in Jesus Christ. But isn't it just like God to take one of His fiercest opponents, a persecutor of the faith, and convert him, changing him into one of the faith's greatest purveyors of the gospel?

It all started with Saul's conviction. While on one of his campaigns of persecution, Saul came across a man by the name of Stephen. Stephen was one of the first deacons chosen by the apostles to perform the work of administrating resources to those in need (see Acts 6). As Stephen was performing his duties, he came in contact with Saul. Saul led a brigade of angry Jewish rioters to stone Stephen to death, but what happened next, I believe, helped the Holy Spirit to sear the conscience of Saul. Stephen was declaring the Word of God with boldness, but the more he spoke, the angrier the crowd became. The crowd eventually stoned him and then took his clothes and robe and laid them at the feet of Saul. As Stephen was being stoned, with the radiant glory of God shining upon his face and looking toward heaven, he saw the face of Jesus, who was sitting at the right hand of the Father. Stephen then looked up and said, "Lord, do not hold this sin against them" (Acts 7:60), and then he died. I believe this display of the power of forgiveness was the beginning of what would become the conversion of Saul.

As Kingdom leaders and those who lead others into innovative change, we, too, must be open to conviction.

As Kingdom leaders and those who lead others into innovative change, we, too, must be open to conviction. Conviction is the act of being brought into accountability for one's actions and deciding to change the situation. For the Kingdom leader, conviction is motivated by the power of the Holy Spirit. The Holy Spirit serves as the moral compass for the leader and governs his actions. When a leader allows himself to be governed by the promptings of the Spirit, all matters of vision, guidance, direction, and correction exist. The leader only moves when prompted by the Spirit. When the leader goes outside of or violates the Holy Spirit's direction, the Spirit convicts or makes the leader aware of his mishap and provides guidance to repentance and restoration.

I believe this is what happened to Saul, and this is what must happen to leaders today if we are serious about bringing innovative change. *People won't change until they see their leader being willing to change,* and change always begins with conviction.

The Conversion of Saul

After receiving permission from the high priest to continue his reign of persecution, Saul found himself on the road to Damascus. As he traveled, he had a divine encounter like he had never experienced before; this encounter was with Jesus Himself. The power of the Holy Spirit (the Spirit of Christ) knocked Saul off his horse, and Saul began to have an intimate conversation with Christ. It went something like this.

> *And he fell to the ground and heard a voice saying to him, "Saul, Saul, why are you persecuting Me?" And he said, "Who are You, Lord?" And He said, "I am Jesus whom you are persecuting, but get up and enter the city, and it will be told to you what you must do." The men who traveled with him stood speechless, hearing the voice but seeing no one. Saul got up from the ground, and though his eyes were open, he could see nothing; and leading him by the hand, they brought him into Damascus. And for three days he was without sight, and neither ate nor drank.*
>
> *Now there was a disciple in Damascus named Ananias; and the Lord said to him in a vision, "Ananias." And he said, "Here I am, Lord." And the Lord said to him, "Get up and go to the street called Straight, and inquire at the house of Judas for a man from Tarsus named Saul, for he is praying, and he has seen in a vision a man named Ananias*

come in and lay his hands on him, so that he might regain his sight." But Ananias answered, "Lord, I have heard from many people about this man, how much harm he did to Your saints at Jerusalem;... But the Lord said to him, "Go, for he is a chosen instrument of Mine, to bear My name before the Gentiles and kings and the sons of Israel; for I will show him how much he must suffer in behalf of My name." So Ananias departed and entered the house, and after laying his hands on him said, "Brother Saul, the Lord Jesus, who appeared to you on the road by which you were coming, has sent me so that you may regain your sight and be filled with the Holy Spirit." And immediately something like fish scales fell from his eyes, and he regained his sight, and he got up and was baptized.

—Acts 9:4–18

It was this divine encounter with Christ that brought about the conversion of Saul. The power of the Holy Spirit not only convicted Saul, but it also prepared his heart for the encounter with Christ. Often, whenever God uses a leader to bring about change, the change is frequently more about bringing change in the leader than change in the setting. God is trying to perfect something in the

God never just changes the followers; He also brings about conversion in the leader.

leader that must be dealt with to bring the leader to a place of conversion and transformation. *The reality is that God never just changes the followers; He also brings about conversion in the leader so the leader will understand conversion and have compassion on the followers when change is needed, either in their individual or collective state of being (setting).* Once Saul had an encounter with Christ, his willingness to submit helped bring about his conversion.

The Consecration of Paul

After his conversion, God took Saul through a season of consecration. What is consecration? The word *consecration* is broken down into two smaller words: *con*, meaning to set aside, and *sacro*, meaning that which is holy. *Consecration* is therefore the setting aside of that which is holy. After his conversion, the Holy Spirit took Saul through a season of consecration.

The text clearly states that after Saul was converted, he lost his sight. The loss of his sight was symbolic of being in the wilderness. The wilderness is frequently analogous to a period of isolation, or being "set aside." Why was this setting aside necessary for Saul? It was necessary to isolate him so that he might be purged from his old nature and purified by the Holy Spirit's indwelling in his new nature. The purging and purifying were essential in preparing him for his next level of service. Acts 9:8–9 states that "Saul got up from the ground, and though his eyes were open, he could see nothing; and leading him by the hand, they brought him into Damascus. And for three days he was without sight, and neither ate nor drank." During this season of darkness, or isolation and dependence, God was able to perfect some things in Saul. The revelation is that sometimes God has to bring us to a place of submission and total dependence, where we have to rely on others to get our attention long enough to engage the consecration process. The other revelation is that leaders must be careful how they intend to bring persecution; it may be in the place of persecution (Damascus) that God brings you to a place of submission and dependence in order to bring you to the place of consecration. All of this was necessary to bring Saul to his ultimate consecration, which was the changing of his name.

Saul's Name Change

Saul's name was changed to Paul. Why was this changing of his name so important? Well, let's first look at the meaning of these names.

Saul

In the original Hebrew, *Saul* means "someone who is asked for or inquired of" from God. This name has a direct correlation in the biblical narrative regarding Israel's first king. God, who had established His covenant with Abraham, desired to be Israel's king (1 Samuel 8–10). While other nations had human kings, God desired this particular designation and position for Himself. He desired to be all that Israel needed. He desired to be their Protector, Provider, Defender, Sustainer, Director, and everything else they might need, that they didn't even know they needed, from a king. Because of their insistence on having an earthly king, God granted them their request and allowed them to "ask for," or choose, their own king. Thus came the name *Saul*. In essence, the people were asking for someone to take God's place in their nation. *Saul* could, therefore, mean "one who takes the place of God." There is great danger in trying to take God's place. Saul found this to be the case in the Old Testament, in 1 Samuel 15. In this text, Samuel instructed Saul to do two things: first, not to touch the things of God for the sacrifice, and second, to destroy all people, beasts, and materials when God gave the Israelites the victory. Saul disobeyed in both instances, and God tore the kingdom from him. Never try to take God's place!

From Saul to Paul

The Saul of the New Testament found himself trying to take God's place as he persecuted the church. He defied the move of God's Spirit on the day of Pentecost and determined to rid Israel of the followers of Christ, but then something happened: Saul had an encounter with Christ. During this encounter on the road to Damascus, Saul was converted, and God changed his nature.

God also changed his name from Saul—"one who takes the place of God"—to Paul—"one who walks in humility." The change in both name and character were essential for Paul's new commission to lead the church and advance the Kingdom of God. As leaders, we must be willing never to try to take God's place, but we must allow God to take us through conversion experiences, both initially and ongoing. Many times, we act like Saul and attempt to take Christ's ministry into our own hands. As chosen vessels, however, we must constantly walk in a state of humility and obedience to be in a position to be used by Him!

The Co-Laboring of Paul

After Paul's conviction, conversion, and consecration, God prepared him for his intended purpose: to establish both the work and doctrine of the church, for the ages, by calling and sending leaders to advance the Kingdom. Paul knew, however, that he could not do this by himself. He knew it would take a concerted effort if the church was to come to fruition and if the work of ministry was to exist beyond his own time. To do this, Paul understood the significance of co-laboring.

Co-laboring is the act of involving others in ministry. It is the process by which leaders engage others in fulfilling a cause bigger than themselves. It simply means to work together. For Paul, it was the process by which churches throughout Asia Minor would be planted and established. While he knew initially that the vision had been given to him, Paul realized that he could not execute this vision by himself. As he was sent out, he took partners along with him who would help him survey the land and plant and establish new churches for Christ's cause. He used a five-step process for co-laboring: identification, equipping, modeling, empowerment, and deployment.

Identification

Identification is the process of establishing who or what something or someone is. For the Kingdom leader, it is the process by which one becomes aware of those around them to discover the unique gifts and abilities one may possess to further the work of the Kingdom. Identification is one of the hallmark qualities of any leader. A good leader is one who always looks for qualities in others for two reasons: first, to assess the qualities of the individual, and second, to look for someone to train to ultimately take the leader's place.

For Paul, identifying others to join him in the work of planting and establishing churches was critical. Paul understood that he needed people with unique qualities, which he might or might not have possessed himself, but which were essential to performing certain tasks for the work of the Kingdom. Paul, the writer of the New Testament books that helped the church to understand the importance of spiritual gifts, knew better than anyone how important it was to find those believers who possessed those gifts. He, therefore, spent time seeking out men and women who could execute the matters of the Kingdom. He chose Barnabas, Apollos, Silas, John Mark, Timothy, Phoebe, Prisca, Priscilla and Aquila, Titus, Tychicus, Luke, Euodia, and Philemon. It is believed that Paul had a network of Christian brothers and sisters of approximately eighty to ninety people who were considered to be his co-laborers.

These people assisted Paul in his work by preaching, teaching, hosting church gatherings, reconciling problems, meeting Paul's needs while in prison, and transcribing his letters. In eight of the thirteen letters Paul is credited with authoring, mention of other names are listed. Paul's letters were a collaborative enterprise and an interchange of ideas and traditions between Paul, his secretaries, and his co-writers, from Timothy to Tertius. All of these and other co-laborers were needed to advance the work of the Kingdom, and Paul brought them to the work by first identifying them. Identification is critical to the life and work of every "PotChanger."

Equipping

After Paul identified his co-laborers, he then equipped them for the work of the Kingdom. The word *equip* is a rather interesting term. The Greek word for *equip* is *katartismos*. It means to "set straight that which was broken." It was a term used by physicians to describe the process of setting a bone after a break. For Paul, equipping meant training leaders by identifying their gifts and abilities and setting them "in order" to be prepared to perform the work of ministry, or to meet the needs of the church and community. Equipping or setting the gifts in order is essential for any innovative change leader. The leader responsible for charting the course for ministry cannot allow his time to be consumed with the mundane things of ministry. However, at first the leader may have to model the behaviors and actions to those who are to carry out the assignments; he has to equip others to perform the ministry that others can do so that he can focus on the things that only he can do. Equipping entails a very important process that prepares people to carry out or perform the various aspects of ministry: This process is called modeling.

Modeling

Modeling is the process of allowing those being trained to mirror the actions of the teacher. Modeling is important because it helps to give the student an actual glimpse, through human interaction, of what a process or concept should look like. There are examples in the Bible of men and women who accepted the responsibility of mentoring others by practicing modeling, as a part of their leadership development, for the students who were following them. From Moses mentoring Joshua, to Elijah mentoring Elisha, to David mentoring Solomon, to Naomi mentoring Ruth, to Daniel mentoring Shadrach, Meshach, and Abednego, they were known for their passion for providing leadership to their students through precept and example. Modeling is so important because it helps the student avoid pitfalls they might ordinarily fall into, had it not been for the mentor's modeling provided to them.

Other than Jesus, Paul is considered to be one of the greatest prototypes of ministry modeling. He took the time to provide instruction, direction, and advice to the men and women of God who had been placed under his care and called to the task of birthing new churches and advancing the Kingdom of God in the early church formation. Let's look at what Paul said to Timothy about what he and Timothy were called to do as mentors and modelers. First Timothy 1:1–11 reads:

> *Paul, an apostle of Christ Jesus according to the commandment of God our Savior, and of Christ Jesus, who is our hope, To Timothy, my true child in the faith: Grace, mercy and peace from God the Father and Christ Jesus our Lord.*

Just as I urged you upon my departure for Macedonia, to remain on at Ephesus so that you would instruct certain people not to teach strange doctrines, nor to pay attention to myths and endless genealogies, which give rise to useless speculation rather than advance the plan of God, which is by faith, so I urge you now. But the goal of our instruction is love from a pure heart, from a good conscience, and from a sincere faith. Some people have strayed from these things and have turned aside to fruitless discussion, wanting to be teachers of the Law, even though they do not understand either what they are saying or the matters about which they make confident assertions. But we know that the Law is good, if one uses it lawfully, realizing the fact that law is not made for a righteous person but for those who are lawless and rebellious, for the ungodly and sinners, for the unholy and worldly, for those who kill their fathers or mothers, for murderers, for the sexually immoral, homosexuals, slave traders, liars, perjurers, and whatever else is contrary to sound teaching, according to the glorious gospel of the blessed God, with which I have been entrusted.

Paul asserts that one of the main goals for him and Timothy was to instruct men and women so that they would not walk in error in understanding and administering the doctrines and discipline of the Kingdom's work and the ministry of Christ. Paul knew there were those in their midst who were teaching unsound doctrine, steeped in heresy and myths, and if allowed, they would continue to profane the things of God and taint the church's work. So Paul took it upon himself to perfect the walk of those following him by setting an example of righteous living through precept and example. He not only told them how to live, but as an expression of the calling placed upon him, he modeled the behaviors of righteousness and obedience and then admonished his followers to do the same. He taught Timothy the importance of modeling such behavior and encouraged Timothy to model the same through precepts and examples. The practice, however, did not stop there. It has been the practice, throughout the ages, for men and women of God to take the examples laid down for them, by those who came before, and to model the same behaviors of righteousness and obedience, so that generations yet unborn would continue to carry on the lineage of becoming faithful men and women of God. It is through the principle of modeling that we, to this day, have become the benefactors of such faithful men and women.

Empowerment

Once followers have been taught the principles of the faith and have been given proper instruction, through precept and example, they must then be empowered to perform the work of the Kingdom. Empowerment is the act of giving one the authority to carry out the assignment's responsibilities in their care. This act does not just happen. It occurs as a result of trustworthiness and faithfulness. Trustworthiness is the act of being worthy of the trust someone in authority places in another to carry out their assignment. As the assignee is faithful to perform the functions given to them, greater trust is established between authority and the assignee. The greater the level of faithfulness, the greater the level of trust is extended to give even greater responsibility. Once the one in authority is confident of the assignee's faithfulness, the next step in the process of multiplication occurs: deployment.

Deployment involves releasing the assignee to fully execute the responsibilities placed on them in the Kingdom.

Deployment

Deployment involves releasing the assignee to fully execute the responsibilities placed on them in the Kingdom. They are given territory of their own in which to fulfill the assignment and begin the process of operating in full authority to model the attributes of leadership of identification, equipping, empowerment, and deployment themselves. They are identified, equipped, empowered, and deployed to seek others to fulfill the same process they have become faithful to do themselves. This is the key to multiplication in ministry and Kingdom increase. This is not just a model to use in the church; it is a model that can be employed in every area of business, if we are concerned about building capacity to meet the demands of those we serve. This is the model Paul employed as he sought to plant churches and expand the bounds of Christendom, and it is the model we are called to employ, if we are to win the world for Christ and expand the boundaries of the Kingdom. Paul is the prototype for church planting and Kingdom expansion. If God can take a persecutor of Christians and use him for His glory, He can use me and you! More importantly, Paul became and remains one of the most significant personalities of the New Testament. Why? Because Paul built a legacy. He became a spiritual father to many and constantly identified, sought after, and poured into the lives of his followers. Now, two thousand–plus years later, he is still making a significant impact in the lives of followers of Christ!

Paul and all of the others mentioned in this chapter are great examples of innovative change leaders who used their wisdom, gifts, and abilities to effect change, impact communities, transform lives, and impart those changes to their generation as well as future generations.

Chapter Four

The Spirit of Adventure

We've discussed innovative change, its importance, and the need to effectively implement it, and we've outlined what an innovative change leader looks like. We now move to a very important aspect of the innovative process. We must ask several fundamental questions: First, how does an innovative change leader know when it's time to change? Second, what are mitigating factors that necessitate change? And third, what are the essential factors needed to initiate and execute innovative change? These and other questions can be answered as we explore and engage the spirit of adventure.

The Spirit of Adventure

An innovative change leader needs to embody the most important element to assist those they lead with moving into new territory; this is the spirit of adventure. The spirit of

Leadership mix helps to foster leadership capital that breeds a culture of organizational trust with their followers. It is the leadership mix and organizational trust.

adventure is the leader's ability, through their evolution and maturity, to rise above established systems and processes and search for an ideal innovative mix that will both inspire and empower their followers to risk exploring uncharted territory. It is the innovation mix of the leader's *Spiritual Integrity, Cultural and Internal Sensitivity, Global Discernment, Hospitable Engagement,* and *Progenitorial Empowerment* that allows them to be freed of a reliance on existing structures and paradigms to explore new and possibly more relevant structures and processes that will meet current and future needs. It is the act of gaining wisdom from past principles, methods, and experiences and possessing a spirit of exploration that allows them to be open to new, more relevant practices and processes. This leadership mix helps to foster leadership capital that breeds a culture of organizational trust with their followers. It is the leadership mix and organizational trust that creates an atmosphere that propels organizational innovative change.

As was mentioned earlier in chapter three, the innovative change leader acquires and embodies five essential innovative change traits that prepares them to create a spirit of adventure. They must always be ready to exhibit the ability to have: **1) Spiritual Integrity**—like Elijah, they will learn how to rely on the power of God to lead them into all situations; **2) Cultural and Internal Sensitivity**—like Jesus, they will learn to have a keen cultural perspective on their setting and intrinsic core values that keep them grounded; 3) Global Discernment—like the sons of Issachar, they will understand the signs of the times, and they will always look for cutting-edge ways to serve those in and beyond their setting; **4) Hospitable Engagement**—like Barnabas, they will look for opportunities to fellowship with and encourage other innovative change leaders; and 5) Progenitorial Significance—like Paul, they will seek opportunities to identify, nurture, and develop future change leaders to foster the spirit of adventure and cultivate a legacy of leadership succession. These essential traits assist the leader in building the necessary leadership capital to forge innovative change. What is leadership capital? The leader consistently and reliably displays the character traits necessary to gain the trust of their followers. The more capital the leader invests, the more capital the leader will have at their disposal when making an innovative change withdrawal. The more the followers see the leader transform into being consistent in executing and modeling the essential innovative change traits, the more willing the followers will be to become vulnerable to the leader's guidance and direction. Igniting and instituting cultural systemic change is found in the leader's ability to create so much capital that those following will be willing to grant the leader permission to take them to places they've never been before.

To sum up the notion of the spirit of adventure, we turn to the late Edwin Friedman, who describes this spirit of adventure in his book *A Failure of Nerve*. He wrote:

> *Conceptually stuck systems cannot become unstuck simply by trying harder. For a fundamental reorientation to occur, that spirit of adventure which optimizes serendipity and which enables new perceptions beyond the control of our thinking processes must happen first.*

The leader's conviction of their beliefs in the change process should be so great that they accomplish their mission with joy and passion. The conviction becomes contagious, and their followers model the passion of their leader. What Friedman is telling us is that the leader who can build leadership capital by building up the people and gaining credibility through precept and practice, while modeling a consistent lifestyle of integral behavior and executing it with joy and passion, is the innovative change leader who can convince followers to take a journey with them that they would not have dared to take with others in the past. The leader must acquire so much capital that the people are willing to both risk and forsake the comfort of the past practices and explore new possibilities and ways of doing things.

The Spirit of Adventure Creative Process

Once the leader has convinced their followers to embrace the spirit of adventure and explore new ways of doing things, they must then navigate them through a discovery process, called the Spirit of Adventure Creative Discovery Process.

The Spirit of Adventure Creative Discovery Process

Every new idea that charts a new direction and shapes a generation begins with a creative discovery process. The creative discovery process is the act of taking followers through a series of discovery steps, which build upon previously evolved steps, eventually bringing them to an aha moment that transforms their thinking toward a preconceived notion, or an established norm, to a new way of thinking and doing. From the Age of Discovery and the invention of the printing press by Johannes Gutenberg, to the travels of Columbus and Amerigo Vespucci's discovery of the Americas, to the discovery of the positive and negative elements in the flow of electricity by Benjamin Franklin, to Thomas Savery's invention of the steam engine, to the invention of the automobile by Carl Benz, Henry Ford, Jean

Joseph Étienne Lenoir, and others, and the discovery of blood plasma by Dr. Charles Drew, each new insight began with the person following a series of steps, which built upon previously evolved steps, eventually bringing them to an aha moment that transformed their thinking toward a preconceived notion, or an established norm, to a new way of thinking and doing. The principle helps us to understand that every invention or new development occurs as the result of an innovative creative process that emanates from a desire to accommodate a generational need.

The Innovation to Accommodate Generational Needs

What is a generational need? Before we define this phrase, we must first clarify what a *generation* is. A *generation* is a group of people born and living at about the same time, regarded collectively. It can also be described as the average span of time from birth to adolescence to adulthood. During this time, children are born, grow up, become adults, and have children of their own. Thirty is considered the dividing age between one generation and the next. Over the past century, there have been approximately six generations. They are as follows:

- **The Great Generation (1898–1928):** This is also known as the GI Generation. This was the first generation to face a global war (WWI), and they lived through both the Roaring Twenties and the Great Depression. This was a generation who witnessed rationing and national patriotism. They were very frugal and understood the importance of "saving for a rainy day."

- **The Builder Generation (1929–1946):** The Builder Generation was the generation who had to "pick up the pieces" after the Great Depression. They not only experienced the aftermath of the Great Depression, but they also experienced the second world war (WWII), as well as the invention and devastation of the atomic bomb.
- **The Boomer Generation (1947–1964):** What happens when soldiers return from a long war and reunite with their significant others? They make babies! Thus, the name for this generation: the baby boomers! At the time, this generation became the largest ever (forty-two million in America). Along with this boom of children came an economic boom. Because there was a sudden deluge of children, new schools had to be built. New homes became a necessity for growing families. And because homes were in all sorts of different neighborhoods, people needed transportation, which spawned the need for

automobile manufacturers to build new plants to produce more cars, and on and on. This was the first generation to experience television on a large scale, and they were the first generation in modern times to witness the assassination of an American president and the signing of new civil rights legislation and national desegregation.

- **The Buster Generation (1965–1980):** Also known as Generation X, this generation witnessed some of the greatest advances in technology. They witnessed the landing of the first human on the moon, the widespread use of the computer, and the invention of transistors and urban renewal. They also witnessed some of America's darkest hours. This generation witnessed the resignation of an American president, the assassination of several great leaders, race riots in major cities, the Vietnam War, and the rise of the drug wars. This generation took a back seat to the baby boomers and has been considered by many as the lost, or minimized, generation.
- **The Millennial Generation (1981–1995):** This generation gets its name because these children ushered in the new millennium. Also known as Generation Next or Generation Y, they became the largest generation ever (with ninety-two million in America). It has been

said that this generation has never been shy or timid about asking questions. This generation witnessed the invention of Macintosh, the first home computer. They witnessed the birth of video games, the integration of the World Wide Web (www), and the "global village" assimilation. They also experienced the creation of twenty-four-hour broadcasting and news cycles, the tearing down of the Berlin Wall, the Soviet Union's dismantling, and the devastating consequences of Acquired Immune Deficiency Syndrome, better known as AIDS. This generation has changed how the world processes information and how we view work and play. They have reconstituted their grandparents' morals and continue to seek to change how we care for and protect our environment.

- **Generation Z (1996–2010):** This generation is still evolving and promises to be more adventurous than all other previous generations. This generation has seen significant advances in technology and how we communicate and engage one another. They witnessed the birth of portable computing through smartphones, laptops, iPads, iPhones, Androids, and tablets. They've witnessed the birth of telepresence and cloud-based computing. They were the first to witness video conferencing and social networking, from MySpace to Facebook, Twitter, Snapchat, and

Instagram. They would rather text than talk, and meet you via FaceTime, Google Hangout, or on their timeline than meet you in person. They've witnessed the rise of online shopping and a global pandemic. Cloud sourcing is a way of life for them, and almost every one of them carries a mobile device with them at all times.

Six generations of people, all living at the same time, each with their own distinct generational nuances. The question is: How can you minister/serve all of them at the same time? The answer: Through innovative change!

- **Generation Alpha (2010–2025):** Presently there are nine thousand Gen Alpha babies born every day. The oldest ones in this generation are ten years old, and the youngest have yet to be born. They are the first generation entirely born within the twenty-first century. The kids of Gen Alpha are growing up in a variety of living arrangements. A large percentage of Alphas are spending at least part of their early formative years in living arrangements that do not include both of their biological parents. "Generation Alpha will be the most formally educated generation ever, the most technology-supplied generation ever, and globally the wealthiest generation ever." More than 2.5 million Alphas are born every week worldwide, and by 2025, they are estimated to number at least two billion. Generation Alpha is the first generation to spend their entire life immersed in technology. They are being shaped by their experiences with Artificial Intelligence. When it comes to spending and making buying choices, they are the decision makers, or at the least, powerful influencers with their parents. A big influence on them is their favorite Instagram or YouTube star. Fifty-five percent say they would purchase a product if they saw their favorite Instagram or YouTube star wearing or using it. Televisions are still the most common way for kids ages six to twelve to watch their favorite shows. And as televisions continue to get "smarter" and more interactive, large-screen televisions are as relevant as they have ever been. Fifty-three percent of Alpha kids have a smartphone by the age of eleven. Gaming is the number-one smartphone activity, followed by watching videos and texting. They expect things on demand. They are being wired to have access to all content anywhere and at any time. They expect instant gratification. Typing is out for them—talking is in. Voice-activated devices are replacing typing. Smart devices are becoming a greater part of family life. The use of devices like the Amazon Dot are growing daily. Thirty-nine percent of Alpha kids use this type of device every week. They are growing up with the familiar voice of Siri, Alexa, and Google Assistant in their homes. This newest American generation displays unprecedented diversity in almost every dimension one can examine: ethnicity, nativity, income, and family arrangements, says Elwood Carlson, demographer and sociology professor.

Generational Needs

As we have seen, generations often forge identities of their own, based upon society's evolution and its needs during that time. As each generation evolves, it begins to foster the theory of innovation. Each generation takes lessons learned from previous generations, integrates new processes and lessons learned, and improves upon them, based upon the desire to fulfill a need for that generation that was never presented before. Therefore, a generational need is an essential requirement desired to fulfill or enhance a specific age group's wants or desires to make life better.

For innovation to be achieved, change leaders must envision.

Innovation Necessitates Vision

For innovation to be achieved, change leaders must envision. The *Oxford Dictionary* defines *vision* as the ability to think about or plan the future with imagination or wisdom. A visionary leader can take previous experiences and imagine and build upon them in new, more pragmatic ways. Vision is the taking of a theory or concept and the shaping of it into a moldable, workable solution. The Bible is very clear on the importance of vision. Proverbs 29:18 reads, "Where there is no vision, the people perish" (KJV). In the New American Standard Version, it reads, "Where there is no vision, the people are unrestrained." The translation that brings it home is the New Living Translation, which reads, "When people do not accept divine guidance, they run wild." The Hebrew word *para'* means "to perish." *Para'* was the word used to describe the movement of a woman's hair. When her hair was not constrained by some form of tie or covering, it blew in whatever direction the wind was blowing. Whether they are churches or businesses, the problem with many organizations is that they are led by managers who have no vision. And when there is no vision, there is no direction; the workers flow in whatever direction the wind is blowing at that time.

An innovative change leader, however, leads her organization with a great level of intentionality. She observes the nuances of the various generations and the key elements that need to be addressed to bring relevance. She imagines better, more pragmatic ways to perform a task, then creates systems or ideas to help to accomplish the task and clearly articulates the process to accomplish the task to her followers. Once the leader employs these principles, she then embodies them in how the work is executed. The process goes something like this:

- **Relevance ignites movements:** Eight minutes and forty-six seconds. That is the amount of time that passed as the world witnessed a cruel and unusual act of police brutality and the life of George Floyd slipped away. Others had experienced police brutality in the past, but this seemed to be the tipping point that would cause communities worldwide to protest that BLACK LIVES MATTER! Almost immediately, from the NFL to NASCAR, from corporate boardrooms to countries around the world, a movement was ignited that changed history, because human life—all human life, including black human life—matters. Whenever any cause takes on a relevance that touches the collective hearts of people, movements are ignited. The majority of movements, however, cannot be fabricated; they must be organic. They must spring from a place of meeting a deeply felt need and ignite a passion for change. In this case, it was the need to change the plight of racial inequality and counter police brutality. In the case of the #MeToo movement, it was the deeply felt need to protect the rights of sexually victimized women. Regardless of the cause, the reality is that relevance connects to deeply felt needs that ignite movements.

- **Movements drive culture:** Whenever movements are ignited, they shape the culture. To be relevant means to bring importance to a matter at hand. It deals with what one is facing right now and how to connect what's happening to a wider audience. Relevance cannot be dealt with in the past. When it is relegated, it no longer speaks to the current state and situation of the setting. There used to be a time when people were tolerant of irrelevance; they went along with the flow. Times, however, have changed the landscape of the culture. People no longer settle for irrelevance because they have seen how present-day systems can meet their needs. They won't settle for an outdated method that no longer meets their needs when they can go across the street and find a method that satisfies their every whim. Why settle for Kmart when Walmart is right across the street? People therefore look for ways to make their environments more meaningful to their everyday existence. Organizations must therefore look for ways to bring relevance to those they serve, understanding that relevance drives culture.

- **Cultures demand change:** A relevant culture will not remain in the same place; it demands that things change. Everything must change; nothing remains the same. Just look at yourself in the mirror and compare your image today with your image five years ago. Everything must change, including organizations! Organizations that remain sensitive to this truth are the ones that operate in a spirit of adventure. They are willing to put in the work to create innovative-change systems to meet the demands of an ever-changing culture. When culture ceases to change, it ceases to be relevant. When it ceases to be relevant, it accelerates its demise. Relevant cultures demand change.
- **Change inspires vision:** Relevance is the motivating factor to change. And change always searches for more effective ways to be relevant. Sometimes that change requires thinking beyond one's level of exposure; we must think outside of the box. Thinking outside of the box requires vision. It is the act of thinking beyond the ordinary. Innovative agents of change are visionary leaders. They look for new and fresh ways to rethink the past's actions to meet the present needs of the culture.
- **Vision births innovation:** Vision always looks for ways to do things better. It takes what already

exists and looks for ways to make it more effective: That is called innovation. Without innovation, the Wright Brothers would have been all we ever knew about aviation. Without innovation, Henry Ford and the Model T would have been all we ever knew about automotive transportation. Innovation always improves on the past and moves us forward to make things better.

- **Innovation explores ideas:** Innovation almost always creates the need to establish processes to bring the innovation to pass. This is the time for team members to think creatively to find new, more efficient ways to execute and perfect existing processes.
- **Ideas establish systems:** It is not enough to have established processes; organized practices, called systems, are needed to create a culture of efficiency. Processes are taken and placed into systems that become the standard for how an organization does business. Once processes have been identified and organized, they are placed into protocols that create effectiveness and efficient systems.
- **Systems shape traditions:** Tried-and-true processes that have stood the test of time, that have become reliable and trustworthy, become the foundations that establish lasting traditions. Traditions are normally

passed from one generation to the next. It may be the family's favorite recipe, or a timeless ritual that has been passed down.

- **Traditions stabilize societies:** One of the key elements needed to create organizational stability and consistency lies in the ability to have tried-and-true processes that have stood the test of time. These tried-and-true traditions are the cornerstones for building long-lasting cultures of innovation. People look for things that are reliable and trustworthy. The reason traditions help to stabilize societies is because generations of people, or organizations, have relied on their timeless integrity.

Societies bring about the change necessary to meet the generational need. True and lasting innovation comes out of an organization's willingness to be relevant. They never settle for or get stuck in present-day traditions for traditions' sake. They realize that traditions do not drive culture; culture is driven by an organization's need to fulfill a generational inquiry that is deeply felt. Innovative organizations will always be agile enough to make the pivot and bring about change when generational inquiry necessitates it. And this process always begins with an organization's need to be relevant. However, the reason that generational needs often go unmet is because organizations underestimate the importance of original intent.

The Power of Original Intent

My wife once had a pair of casual shoes that she loved dearly. She would wear them every leisurely chance she got, because the shoes were comfortable and easy to wear. After a time, though, she grew weary of the shoes, and she would kick them off at the door upon entering the house from the garage. Eventually she misplaced the shoes and stopped wearing them. The shoes became a doorstop for the pantry. One day, my wife opened the pantry, spotted those once-favorite shoes, and wondered aloud what they were doing in the pantry. Someone replied that they were being used as a doorstop. My wife replied by saying, "If someone had just asked me, you would have understood the original intent of the shoes. They weren't made for stopping; they were made for wearing."

What is the moral of this story? Be careful about jumping to conclusions. One day you may discover that the thing that once gave you comfort has now become a doorstop. People frequently make false or inaccurate assumptions about things because they do not understand their original intent.

Original intent is the process by which we understand why something exists in the first place. In legal terms, it is called the *spirit of the law.* It involves understanding why something was created and the setting from which it evolved. There is another legal term that can convolute the process of intent: the *letter of the law.* The letter of the law is a literal application based upon an individual interpretation. There is a danger in operating in the letter of the law when you do not understand the law's spirit. It may cause you to misinterpret the application of a law and thereby misapply its meaning. That is why a good lawyer always goes back to look for precedent. *Precedent* is the act of using an earlier event or action that is regarded as an example or guide to be considered in subsequent similar circumstances.

You may be asking what this legal term has to do with how you can usher in innovative change in your organization or church. I believe that chaos and confusion exist in churches and other organizations because people do not take the time to research original intent. I also believe this is the reason churches and organizations remain stuck in a process, system, or tradition: They never fully understood precedent.

Innovative organizations must operate with a spirit of adventure.

Before you begin the process of innovation, or any kind of change, make sure you first understand precedent and original intent. It could mean the difference between having a successful launch of an innovative idea, or the crash of an ill-prepared vision, system, or process.

Innovative organizations must operate with a spirit of adventure. When integrity, successful track records, and meaningful relationships are established and nurtured, organizations will build congregational trust to drive innovative change. Movements, cultures, vision, ideas, systems, traditions, and stabilized societies also help foster the proper adventure mix to spawn necessary change. Finally, understanding the original intent of a product, program, or tradition will help minimize confusion and set out the authentic purpose and reason for being for the ongoing usage of systems, or the appropriate termination of a thing. All these things working together help to set up an environment for healthy and effective innovative change.

Chapter Five

One Ingredient That Inspires Innovative Change: Trust

> The first job of a leader—at work or at home—is to inspire trust. It's to bring out the best in people by entrusting them with meaningful stewardships, and to create an environment in which high-trust interaction inspires creativity and possibility.
>
> —Stephen M.R. Covey, *The Speed of Trust*

Inspiring Trust

As the above quote from Stephen M.R. Covey suggests, one of the most effective attributes in an innovative leader's tool bag that helps motivate and bring about meaningful and lasting innovative change is trust. *Trust* is defined as the firm reliability, ability, or strength of someone or something. It is the act of relying on the character, conduct, and integrity of a person or thing to act in a certain way or to perform a specific task. The greater the reliability, the deeper the trust; the greater the trust, the greater the speed of bringing about innovative change.

Organizations often miss the importance of trust. They feel that if people have vision and understand the reason for change, they will readily accept and adhere to it. This, however, is not always the case. Individuals become attached to vision, concepts, practices, or traditions because the organization took the time to inspire them by informing and selling them on the idea. They established trust, and shared a sense of ownership, because the people were brought into the decision-making process. They felt valued and that their voices mattered; they were inspired. Unless they feel the same levels of inspiration regarding ownership and buy-in, when changes are made, their reaction will oftentimes come in the form of pushback because they have not been inspired about the change. Trust must be earned, and people must be inspired; people need to feel secure when investing their human capital and life's energy into systems, processes, and traditions.

The best way to allay their fears is by building trust and showing the reliability of the innovative change. Anything short of this will almost always fail the project or idea. One might ask the question: Why is the act of building trust so important? The answer is because the level of trust will almost always determine the speed of change. If there is no trust, there is no change. However, understanding how building trust works will help leaders inspire followers to move from doubt and suspicion to ownership and buy-in. To answer this question, we must first understand how trust is destroyed and what is needed to build, or reestablish, it.

The Age of Cynicism

We are living in the greatest era for information that has ever existed. Not since the printing press has such a deluge of information impacted the lives of people. Wherever we turn, we are bombarded by information. From twenty-four-hour news cycles, to social media, to the Internet, unfathomable amounts of information are at our fingertips. Search engines such as Google, Bing, and Yahoo vie for every moment of our attention. Siri and Alexa have become our best friends as they use artificial intelligence (AI) to meet our needs, even before we ask. And although we are living in the great information era, most of us are in information overload.

The danger of having so much information at our fingertips is that people begin to question everything; no one trusts anyone anymore, and everyone seems to be cynical. We are living in the age of cynicism. Cynicism is an attitude characterized by a general distrust of others' motives.[8] The deluge of information has changed how people respond to one another. There is a tendency now, in our culture, to mistrust before trusting. There used to be a time when people would give one another the benefit of the doubt. People lived by the notion that most people were inherently good and that their word was their bond; you were innocent until proven guilty. Now you're convicted in the public square before you even have an opportunity to defend yourself.

There is no greater example of the prevalence of cynicism than in American culture. The culture of trust that once made the United States a bastion of patriotism has given in to "alternative facts" and "fake news." The culture of cynicism has led to the democratization of the media in America. In an article dated April 27, 2016, *Forbes* magazine posted the results of a survey conducted by the American Press Institute, which stated that only 6 percent of Americans had a great deal of confidence in the news media.

Further, *Five-Thirty-Eight*, in its December 17, 2019, edition entitled "In American Politics, Everyone's a Cynic," published a survey taken from the American National Election Survey that the public trust index in government

---

8 Luis E. Navia (1996). *Classical Cynicism: A Critical Study*. Contributions in Philosophy. Greenwood Publishing Group, p. 1.

has plummeted from 52 percent in 1964 to 17 percent in 2016.[9] Pew Research also stated that fifty years ago, during the presidency of Lyndon B. Johnson, the trust index for elected officials was 77 percent.[10] In a January 11, 2019, article entitled "America's Most & Least Trusted Professions," *Forbes* showed that nurses had the highest level of respect, at an 84 percent trust level, while members of Congress had only an 8 percent trust level.[11]

The erosion of trust in the political system has caused an erosion of trust in other areas of society, thus creating an environment for cynicism to flourish. This erosion has also permeated corporate and faith cultures. The level of trust between executives and employees, or between pastors and parishioners, has eroded in recent years. The same *Forbes* study showed that the trust level of clergy in 2019 was 37 percent, and 17 percent for business executives. What can corporations and congregations do to restore trust within their cultures? They must create environments that foster trust and care between their employees and their congregants,

---

9 See https://fivethirtyeight.com/features/in-american-politics-everyones-a-cynic/.

10 See https://www.pewresearch.org/politics/2019/04/11/public-trust-in-government-1958-2019/.

11 See https://www.forbes.com/sites/niallmccarthy/2019/01/11/americas-most-least-trusted-professions-infographic/#75fa42637e94.

respectively. One way to foster a new environment is through processes of trust.

Processes of Trust

Systemic and lasting change does not occur as a result of gaining information and knowledge. If that were the case, then whenever new information is introduced to a body of people, institutional change should occur organically. However, that has never been the case, whether in the age of the printing press of the sixteenth century or the digital revolution age of the twenty-first century. If information was the driving force behind change, then change would take place all around us, at all times. If knowledge and information are not the driving forces behind change, what is? It is the act of engaging our emotional processes of trust, which initiates building and establishing lasting change. Processes of trust are systems developed to foster trust within an established environment. These systems can be integrated into any organization's culture. These processes aim to change the cultural ethos to promote and facilitate an ongoing spirit of trust among all members.

The reason leaders and organizations have so much difficulty with change is because of their lack of trust and fear of the unknown. People would rather remain in a familiar pool of water, which will ultimately drown them, than to run the risk of walking a new path that will lead them to dry land. People typically hate journeying into the unknown. Further, if they have no confidence in those who are attempting to lead them into the unknown, they are especially reluctant to follow. We are creatures of habit; we love being in familiar environments. Whether they are people, places, or objects, familiar things give us a sense of comfort and security. Anything that threatens that sense of security can usher in a sense of trauma. *Trauma* is defined as a deeply distressing or disturbing experience. There are different types of trauma, including emotional, mental, and spiritual trauma. Whenever unexpected change occurs, the change can disrupt our places of security. These disruptions, without any warning or ability to prepare for the disruption, can become traumatic events. The compounding of traumatic events can cause a person to become traumatized, which is the act of remaining in a place of ongoing trauma. Unless methods are employed to erase the traumatic occurrences' negative effects, the individual can become nihilistic and lose any hope of escaping the environment, which in turn fosters additional trauma. Any event that resembles the traumatic episode may trigger the individual and cause them to emotionally regress into a previous traumatic moment. One effective method of dealing with trauma is emotional process.

Emotional Process

Emotional Process is a family systems theory used in psychotherapy with people who have experienced instances of trauma. Whether it was trauma experienced while in the field of battle, trauma experienced during domestic violence, trauma experienced due to street shootings and killings, trauma experienced through police profiling and brutality, or trauma experienced as a result of sexual molestation or child abuse, all result in ingrained impulses of emotional fright and fear that the same thing will happen again, or will happen to them. Emotional Process Theory supposes that exposure to similar effects, in a safe environment, can alter the relationships between the fear stimulus and these networks. For this to happen, the network must first be activated, and then new information must be encoded that is different from what was in the initial fear network. When the victim is repeatedly exposed to similar fears in a "control" environment, with the results being positive and securing affirmations, it is believed that the previous fear stimuli will be abated and replaced by stimuli of peace, assurance, and trust.

Individual and Congregational Trauma

In my dealings with doctoral students over the past fifteen-plus years, I have discovered striking similarities between students and settings. Many of them have dealt with various forms of dysfunction and trauma, in both their personal and their professional lives. I have discovered that some of the most gifted church leaders, those who are leading thousands of congregants, have had to deal with traumatic issues during their lifetimes. From dysfunctional families, to an absence of affection, to substance abuse by their parents, domestic violence, child abuse, and even sexual molestation, many church leaders have struggled with hidden secrets that have left indelible stains in their souls. While many have sought therapy to help them overcome these challenges, many others are still stuck in the mire of past experiences that have debilitated them in various areas of their lives and ministries. The tragic irony is that this disease of trauma doesn't stop with the leader. Many members have experienced the same dysfunctions their leaders encounter. Some seek help, but the majority keep brushing these issues under the rug of their soiled past. And when you connect a damaged pastor with a congregation full of damaged people, the atmosphere promotes an ethos of trauma, hurt, fear, pain, and mistrust.

Organizational Emotional Process

Organizational Emotional Process is the way in which pastor and congregation, or employer and employee, establish a "safe place" that builds affirmation, assurance, and trust for those in the work or faith environment. In short,

Organizational Emotional Process, or OEP, takes the same processes used in family systems therapy and integrates them into the work/faith environment. OEP presupposes that exposure to similar effects can alter the relationships between the fear stimulus and these networks in intentionally created safe environments. For this to happen, the network must first be activated, and then new information must be encoded that is different from what was in the initial fear network. When the victim is repeatedly exposed to similar fears in a "control" environment, with the results being positive and securing affirmations, it is believed that previous fear stimuli will be abated and replaced by stimuli of peace, assurance, and trust.

OEP for a church means establishing "safe zones" and "safe acts," non-threatening environments and behaviors that promote positive affirmations of healing from past congregational hurt, pain, and trauma. The congregation is intentional about developing core values of safety and healing, motivated by the unconditional love of God (*agape* ἀγάπη). When promoted and administered effectively, these become the principles and behaviors that guide every action of the congregation. The greater the reinforcement of "safe zones" and "safe acts," the greater the level of trust and the greater the likelihood of fostering an environment of positive affirmations, security, and innovative change, when necessary.

Once the culture has been primed for building trust, the innovative change leader can implement processes to foster trust by building organizational consensus with the people. *Consensus* is defined as a generally accepted opinion or decision among a group of people. It is the middle ground in decision-making. To share in the consensus-making process, participants must have shared values and goals and be willing to agree on the organization's overall direction. True consensus cannot be achieved until the leader understands the organization's cultural ethos, how organizations think, and how to take the members/followers through the organizational consensus process.

Organizational Consensus Process: Understanding the Dynamics

As each organization has a personality, the ethos, or spirit, of the organizational culture is determined by organizational dynamics. *Dynamics* can be defined as those characteristics that motivate the flow of the organization. How the spirit of the organization acts and reacts is determined by dynamic flows and processes. Much like a family and genograms, which determine a family's personalities and characteristics, organizations also have a dynamic makeup, based upon the organizational history and structure. From top-down hierarchical, to responsibility-based functional, to flat-based horizontal, to center-based divisional, to cross functional-based matrix, to group-based teams, to multilevel-based network structures, organizational structures and flows help drive the dynamics of the organization.[12] Similarly, the dynamics and personalities of churches are determined by the organizational structure, or pattern, of the church. Historically, churches were structured in one of four basic ways as outlined in the article, "Effective Ministry Structures: Organizing for Church Health and Growth."[13]

1. **Episcopal Pattern:** Episcopal government is hierarchal and autocratic (not democratic or representative). It is based on the belief that Christ, as the Head of the church, has entrusted the church's leadership to popes, archbishops, bishops, and pastors, whom they view as the successors of the apostles. Higher-level leaders choose and appoint lower-level leaders. The congregation does not vote anyone into office.

2. **Presbyterian Pattern:** The term *Presbyterian* comes from the Greek word *presbuteros*, which means "elder." Local congregations are not led by a single elder or

---

12 Shannon Williams, Lucidchart Blog, "7 types of organizational structures (+ org harts fro implementation)," https://www.lucidchart.com/blog/types-of-organizational-structures.

13 "Effective Ministry Structures: Organizing for Church Health and Growth," Pastor's Pub, http://www.pastorspub.net/effective-ministry-structures-organizing-church-health-growth/.

pastor, but by a group of elders (known as the "session" [Presbyterian] or "consistory" [Reformed]). The congregation elects the elders. Then, the elders lead the church. The elders have authority in the church as representatives of the congregation. According to Presbyterian polity, there are two types of elders: teaching elders and ruling elders.

3. **Congregational Pattern:** As the name indicates, the final authority in this pattern does not rest with the bishops (Episcopalians) or the elders (Presbyterians), but rather with each local congregation (self-law by each assembly of believers). Congregationalists emphasize the priesthood of all believers.
4. **Nongovernmental Pattern:** This pattern emphasizes the Holy Spirit's ability to lead and guide each believer. As these people see it, external structures usually degenerate into formalism, which quenches the Spirit.

Organizational structures and patterns help to shape the dynamics of the church, thus shaping congregational personality. Organizational personality can help to identify change markers that will determine the success or failure of the change process.

Innovative Change Markers

There are five distinct markers that influence organizational dynamics in innovative change. The direction of these markers will help determine the dynamics that will influence the ultimate decision, whether to change or not. This is critical, because many leaders try to influence change themselves without paying attention to these markers. The markers serve as directional guides as to how the organization will adapt to the proposed changes. When executed correctly, the natural flow of decisions will be organic and emanate from the organization's cultural ethos, resulting in a healthy renewal, or affirmation, of trust. People will, thereby, affirm the decision, resulting in organizational buy-in and support.

The following is how the marker formula influences the process of innovative change. Either the dynamics of the top 25 percent or the bottom 25 percent will determine the idea's fate.

Top 25 Percent

1. **Vision Catchers (10 percent):** These individuals are the first to catch the vision. Often, they are influencers who have connected to the vision of the agent of change and are eager to begin the process of actualizing the vision. They make up approximately 10 percent of the organization.

2. **Embracers (15 percent):** Frequently called early adopters, these individuals take the time to find out (evaluate) the proposed idea, weigh its merits, and make a decision based upon the evidence of the idea's effectiveness and thereby embrace the idea. They comprise approximately 15 percent of the organization. If the first two groupings are sold on the idea, they will serve as important influencers in the dynamics of how the remaining markers will decide.

Bottom 25 Percent (the Vocal Minority)

3. **Rejecters (15 percent):** These individuals have a negative view of the change—not only of this change, but of change in general. They look, with a critical eye, for every way possible to defeat the change. They operate out of their mistrust caused by past hurts and experiences, and they allow their past hurts to determine their perspectives regarding change. They are often connected to a previous vision, tradition, or idea connected sentimentally to a past leader, movement, or process. They want things to remain the same. If change does occur, they will eventually concede and reluctantly accept the change. They comprise 15 percent of the negative dynamic of the organization.
4. **Vision Snatchers (10 percent):** The next marker is the vision snatcher. Whether they were hurt by past

leadership, have never been connected to vision, or have an ulterior motive to destroy the movement, their sole responsibility is to create chaos and confusion around the idea. They will even resort to manipulation and sabotage if allowed to do so. It is possible that they will never agree to, nor accept change. They make up the last 10 percent of the marker mix.

The Middle

(Note: Innovative change is either won or lost in the middle)

5. **Emulators (50 percent):** This group's decision will be determined by the momentum of either the top 25 percent or the bottom 25 percent of the organization. Their actions will serve as the decision that determines the future success or failure of the innovative idea. This group historically sits back and watches the reaction of the influencers. Suppose the reaction of the first 25 percent of markers is positive and affirming, and their decisions help to shape the momentum of the idea in a positive way. In that case, they will move toward the consensus of the first 25 percent of the markers. If the idea does not take off as planned and gain the necessary traction, they will move toward rejecting the innovative idea. Their decision will impact 75 percent of the organization. Any organization with 75 percent of their followers buying

in to the change can successfully implement the new ideas. ***Innovative change is either won or lost in the middle.*** It is critical that the innovative change leader understands this dynamic and how it will affect all organization decisions moving forward.

The leader needs to focus on spending less time with the rejecters and snatchers and more time with the embracers and catchers!

Role of the Innovative Agent of Change
(to win the middle)

The role of the Innovative Change Leader is to win the middle. Frequently, the leader focuses his time on convincing the bottom 25 percent to get on board, while his greatest pathway to success is the top 25 percent. ***The leader needs to focus on spending less time with the rejecters and snatchers and more time with the embracers and catchers!*** The way to win the middle is to equip the *embracers and catchers* with the tools and resources to inform and convince the middle. They must build positive momentum and create a culture of trust, which then creates buy-in with everyone. Leaders must intentionally set aside time to "pour" into the embracers and catchers to make sure they can serve as influencers to lead the change. Leaders must also be cautioned that while they spend time with this group, they should not isolate the other members of the organization.

They must learn how to navigate instruction and influence with wisdom, while affirming the worth of all the members of the organization. This will serve as the formula to motivate those who cannot see to trust those who can, to lead them into and through uncharted territory.

Following this formula and process will help to guarantee the acceptance of ideas that will help to shape and bring about innovative change. Building trust, knowing your organizational culture and structure, and creating a climate for consensus building will help to create a culture of lasting innovative change.

The following is a real-life case study that will help you understand this process better and how it can work in your ministry or business context.

Chapter Six

"Grace 2000": A Case Study

Setting

The setting for this case study is Grace African Methodist Episcopal Zion (A.M.E. Zion) Church in Charlotte, North Carolina. Grace Church was founded in 1886, as twenty-seven former members of Clinton Chapel A.M.E. Zion Church withdrew and formed Grace Chapel, with their motto being "God, Religion, and Temperance."[14] The church experienced tremendous growth during the early part of the twentieth century, and it became a significant part of black leadership and culture in the Charlotte, North Carolina, community. Many of the black community leaders were members of the church, including doctors, lawyers, barbers, beauticians,

---

[14] See http://landmarkscommission.org/wp-content/uploads/2016/11/Grace-A.pdf, p. 5.

police officers, teachers and school administrators, brick masons, and carpenters. Grace also played a significant role in advancing the A.M.E. Zion Church in the South. Seven of its pastors became bishops in the denomination, and several other pastors served as general officers. I was appointed as pastor to lead the congregation in 1990 due to several years of decline during previous pastoral administrations.

When this pastor arrived at the age of thirty-two, the congregation was experiencing a season of low spiritual self-esteem. Not only had the numerical membership declined, so had the upkeep of the building. Upon my initial visit to the property, the plaster was hanging off the walls. This beautiful gothic structure needed significant repair, but the congregation's spirit was such that they had neither the enthusiasm nor the energy needed to make such changes. This energetic pastor, who had worked previously in corporate America and who had served previously as a choir director, was ready and prepared for the task of spiritual renewal and revitalization. On the pastor's first Sunday, thirty-nine people were in attendance, not including the pastor's family. Worship was strictly traditional; the church was proudly known as a "listening" congregation. There was seldom an "amen," and very few reactions to the singing and preaching. The membership roll was 211, and many of the church's members had begun to stray. For the next seven months, this pastor, who was used to the "call and response" of the black church, along with energetic worship during the worship experience, began to integrate his preferred style into the worship experience. The people were reluctant to join in, but as time went on, more and more of the membership began to participate in the worship experience. Members began to return to worship, and the weekly average worship attendance grew to approximately eighty-five. There seemed to be a renewed sense of excitement and expectation returning to the congregation.

Moment of Crisis

One of the observations made during this pastor's first year was the need for more ministry space. Although the edifice was a beautiful gothic structure, no provisions had been made for growth or future ministry development; the church was land locked. In the pastor's haste and immaturity to bring the people along, he began to share ideas about moving the church to another location. This not only brought frustration to the congregation, but it also bred a spirit of rebellion and anger. The City of Charlotte published an article about the future of "downtown." It showed multitiered housing, a light rail, an entertainment complex, and a transportation center. This young pastor, seeing this article and understanding the church's need to move to a more suitable community, began to hastily promote moving the location of the church. This act was both premature and irresponsible. Two things were happening: The pastor didn't understand the congregation's culture, and he had not received the trust of the congregation. He had disrupted the norm and brought in a spirit of distrust, which led to trauma. The congregants liked him, but they had not yet grown to trust and follow him. As a result, two of the church's most highly respected officers wrote a thirteen-page letter voicing their opposition to the pastor's plans, and they sent it to every household in the congregation. The pastor was livid. He was about to react to the letter by punishing them for writing it. The blessing in disguise for the pastor was that several other members pulled him aside and gave him wise counsel. They advised him not to seek retribution, but to find another way to get their attention—and the pastor listened. He had to find a way to restore trust and create an environment of Organizational Emotional Process.

Moment of Reflection

The pastor took the next seven months, during which time he prayed, observed the congregation and culture, sought advice from more wise, mature pastors, listened, prayed, and listened some more. During this time, God began to give him direction and guidance on how to bring the necessary innovative change to the congregation. It wasn't that change didn't need to occur; it just needed to happen in a way that brought clarity, trust, and buy-in to the process.

Moment of Revelation

From this time of prayer, observation, listening, and reflection, God gave revelation. This was the year of 1991. The church was less than ten years away from the turn of the century and the birth of a new millennium. The pastor was instructed to form a team of members to explore the possibilities of what the church could look like in the year 2000. The team was organized, and the project was called *"Grace 2000: A New Century, A New Grace."*

The First Meeting

The pastor took all of November and December in 1991 to communicate individually with each participant he was guided to invite. Everyone he was led to invite graciously accepted the invitation. He even invited one of the two people who had earlier written the letter against him (that was a God move)! The committee met on Monday, January 20, 1992, on the Martin Luther King Jr. holiday. Fifteen participants, plus the pastor, met for six hours, with a short break for lunch. They listened to the pastor's purpose and vision and established their name for the ministry: Vision Planning Ministry.

Vision Planning Ministry

The ministry was comprised of five sub-ministries, namely:

- **Spiritual Growth:** To deal with all matters concerning prayer, worship, evangelism, etc.
- **Physical Growth:** To deal with all matters concerning the present physical structure of the church and any plans for further physical growth and expansion, etc.
- **Discipleship:** To deal with all matters concerning teaching: Bible study, church school, leadership training, catechism, new members' orientation, etc.
- **Audio-Video:** To deal with all matters concerning the sound during worship, the recording of worship, the sharing of recorded materials for purchase, for evangelism and the sick and shut-in, and the presentation of all materials representing the church to both congregants and community, etc.
- **Transportation:** To deal with all matters pertaining to providing means of transportation for the membership and those in the community who were without transportation.

Safe Zone and Safe Acts

The ministry was deemed a "safe zone," where all ideas could be shared as "safe acts," where no one would feel threatened or ostracized by what they shared. This began to build an environment of trust and fellowship among the team members, which ultimately permeated throughout the rest of the congregation. Each sub-ministry was given its initial assignment and a timeline to report its findings. The ministry met each Thursday, for the first three months, and then the third Thursday of each month. Trust, synergy, and comradery were being established, more and more, with each meeting.

The First Presentation

After six months, in July 1992, the ministry prepared to present its initial findings to the congregation in a members' retreat. The pastor spoke of the ministry's overall purpose, and each ministry spoke of its respective purposes and goals. The congregation bought in to the concept of the ministry and the timelines each sub-ministry had established, according to their priorities.

Renovation

It was voted by the congregation that the first major project would be the renovation of the existing facility. Remember, I mentioned earlier that the pastor did not understand the congregational culture. The membership's median age was sixty-seven years old, with a number of retired members in their seventies and eighties. The revelation that came from this observation was that they were more concerned with having a decent place to be funeralized than they were about building a new church. The process began by determining what the renovations would entail. After much debate, the entire facility was renovated to bring the church back to its 1902 luster. A new slate roof was laid, bricks were pointed up and re-mortared, steeples were secured and refurbished, stained-glass windows were re-leaded and enclosed, doors were sanded and varnished, pews and carpet were re-padded, and floors were stripped and waxed/tiled. The entire church was painted from top to bottom, with intricate detail being given to accents on the chair railings and the octagonal ceiling. It was a masterpiece! The renovation estimate was $270,000; the people voted unanimously to move forward on it! Upon completion of the work, I remember an eighty-seven-year-old female member saying, "Y'all can build whatever you want to now, because I've got somewhere I'm proud to be funeralized in!" Trust had been restored because we did with the money what we said we would do. The people were proud and excited, which led to members inviting other guests to church, and the congregation grew out of a greater sense of trust and fellowship. Grace was back!

Relocation

One of the findings from the Physical Growth Ministry was that in order to prepare for future generations, the church needed to relocate to an area where they had space to grow and a population to attract. The Physical Growth Ministry began to conduct demographic studies on growth patterns and city and county plans for future growth. They also began to look at various types of architecture that could be used to accommodate future needs. Surveys were provided to the congregation on the best place to move and the type of architecture they would prefer in the new facility.

The surveys' results came back: The congregation voted to continue to worship in the present facility and to conduct inner-city ministry and relocate the church to the northeast quadrant of the city. They also voted to build a modern-gothic-type structure in a university-styled setting, in phases.

Purchase of the Land

The church began to look for land to purchase. They found a couple of properties and eventually settled on one. This site settled in their spirit. It fell in line with the vision God had given the pastor of one church in two locations (who had heard of that in the early nineties?), with the satellite location worshiping in an elementary school and the main location remaining downtown. There was an elementary school approximately a quarter mile from this parcel of land. When they went to place a bid on the land, someone else had outbid them; the land was off the market. A few months later, the Realtor announced that that deal on the property had fallen through and the church should place another bid. When the church did, however, they were outbid again. You wouldn't believe it, but a few more months passed, and the Realtor announced that the second deal had also fallen through. The church offered a final bid, it was accepted, and the church closed on the property!

One Church in Two Locations

The church began to make plans to worship at the satellite location until the new facility was built. A site crew was created to set up and take down the equipment for the early morning worship service. I will never forget this dedicated group of men and women who labored every Sunday to make sure the school was converted for worship and then reset for school after worship was over. We would have an 8:30 a.m. worship service at the school, then change, drive downtown, and conduct an 11:00 a.m. service. We did this for several years. The satellite church began to grow, and surprisingly, some people from the satellite church began at the downtown location. The satellite church was more laid-back and contemporary in worship, while the downtown church had more of a blended style of worship. Both continued to grow. Every fifth Sunday, we would have joint worship, either at the satellite or downtown location, to bring a sense of fellowship and familiarity between both sites.

The End Result

The result was that the church eventually fulfilled the vision that was laid out. The people captured the vision, dared to trust their leadership, created buy-in, and brought the vision to reality. Both buildings stand today as a testament to what a community working together can do! The other sub-ministries of the Vision Planning Ministry continued to fulfill their missions and added to the depth and growth of the overall ministry. Grace Church became a shining example of what can occur when a leader takes the time to understand the congregational culture and develop a ministry that creates trust, community, vision, cooperation, collaboration, faith, and execution.

Chapter Seven

A Lesson from My Mother

> There is an appointed time for everything. And there is a time for every matter under heaven.
>
> —Ecclesiastes 3:1

I had the pleasure of being raised by a great mother. In addition to being one of the top administrators of education in our community, she was both a tremendous wife and mother. My mother was also a great cook. She had majored in home economics in college and served as the chief dietitian in a hospital before going into the field of education. We were privileged to enjoy some of the greatest cooking around at our own family table. My mother grew up on a farm in South Carolina and learned how to cook from the best, and we enjoyed the fruit of her labors! One secret to good cooking that my mother taught me was to make sure you always had the right pot. The pot's age didn't matter; what mattered most was the purpose of the pot—what the pot was created to do.

Mother had in her arsenal a stainless-steel skillet, a cast-iron skillet, a cast-iron baking pot, and a cast-iron stewing pot, and every now and then she would use an aluminum pan for baking. She had pots for frying, cooking, stewing, and baking, and you had to know which pot was used for what. She had some pots that dated back to her grandmother, and there were others she bought along the way herself. Some were meant to last for generations, and some only lasted through one baking cycle; some had been handed down through the generations, and others were acquired more recently. There were some that she kept, some that she handed down, some that she gave away, and some that she threw away. She didn't get mad when it was time to throw a pot away, because she understood that the pot had served its intended purpose. My mother understood that each pot had its own purpose. Some were meant to be kept, and some were meant to be thrown away. Every one of them must fulfill its intended purpose.

The revelation in this story is that there is a time and place for everything under heaven. Some things have an eternal purpose: They should never change. Some things were never intended to be around forever. The same is true in business and in ministry. As innovative change leaders, we must understand that there are some things in ministry we should not keep, while other things should never change.

Things We Should Not Keep

- **Things kept for the mere sake of sentiment:** While we are emotional creatures and creatures of habit, we must never make decisions for sentimental value only. We must be careful how we allow our feelings about things of the past to impact and determine the path for our future. If something has fulfilled its purpose, either share it with others who may need it or discard it. Never allow such things to remain because they remind you of the good ol' days.
- **Things kept for the mere sake of tradition:** Like keeping things for sentiment only, we must not keep things around just because we've used them out of tradition. While tradition has its place and some things are non-negotiables, we should not allow things of the past to hold us captive just because they worked in another era. Why keep using a wood-fired oven when you can cook more efficiently with electricity or gas? Learn from tradition, but don't allow tradition to bind you.
- **Things kept for the mere sake of relation:** This one gets us in more trouble than most any other. We keep

something around because a relative or a friend passed it down to us. It's amazing how people will use the church as a museum for things they no longer want in their house. I remember pastoring a church (not this one) where someone donated a washer and dryer to the church. Huh? If it's not good enough to be in your house, don't bring it to the church. And just because it gave you great service in your house, do not just bring it to the church. Many other agencies would love to have your hand-me-downs. The church should be a place working for the salvation of souls, not routinely the place for the salvaging of our old housewares.

- **Things kept for the mere sake of religion:** I realize this is a hard one, but don't just keep doing things that were meant for a past generation of worshipers. Don't get me wrong: Some tenets of the faith should never change, like the sacraments of baptism and the Lord's Supper. Reading the announcements during worship or reading the obituary during a funeral is not something that should never change. These were things done in past generations because many people could not read, and someone had to read these things for them. Why do we tell people what's next on the program now, when we have already given them a program? Still, why do we relegate worship to a certain hour when the original time for worship a hundred years ago was created to meet the needs of farmers who had to work the fields before coming to church? Don't keep something just because it worked in the past. Ask yourself: Why does it exist? If it's still relevant today, then consider maintaining it. But if it's not, then decide what you will do with it, but don't paralyze the church of today with antiquated patterns from the past.

Those are things that can and will change, but there are some things that should never change.

Things We Should Never Exchange

- **Essential elements for expediency:** While times and occasions might not warrant expediency, essential elements should never be replaced. Things such as common decency, grace, mercy, prayer, and the ministry of the Word should never be replaced.
- **Principles for practices:** There are certain eternal principles that must always remain. The Ten Commandments are not suggestions; they are commandments. They are eternal principles for life, and so are the Beatitudes.
- **Purpose for personality:** There are temptations in this world that can cause us to turn the spotlight of

personal accomplishments away from God and onto ourselves. We should never mistake our personalities for God's purposes. If you walk according to God's plan for your life, He'll lift you up before the people.

- **Mission for methods:** One of the biggest mistakes churches and organizations make is getting stuck in procedures and methods. While protocols have their purpose, most purposes are for a specific period. If we always focus on the mission of the church rather than the methods of the church, the mission will always be relevant for the times and seasons of the church.
- **Why for what:** One of the most important tools in the leader's toolbox is to understand and ask the question why. When you focus on the why instead of the what, you'll never lose your purpose.

Just as my mother understood that there is a time and season for everything, including pots, innovative change leaders must understand there is a time and season for the ebbs and flows of both business and ministry. There are some things that will remain, and there are some things that will need to either be left, changed, or replaced. May we ever be discerning and intentional about keeping in business and in the church the things that make it relevant and impactful for present generations and generations yet to come.

Chapter Eight

The Significance of Sustainability

We've discovered the power of innovative change, and we've seen, through the case study, how it can transform an organization. We've seen how innovative change leaders, who are sensitive to the culture they serve, can address mistrust and trauma issues by modeling a leadership gift mix of innovative change traits. We've discovered how carrying out this process can help create Organization Emotional Processes that build trust and fellowship, leading to organic and lasting change. These tenets are critical to ongoing organizational health. However, you may ask the question, how do we ensure the sustainability of such a culture for present and future generations? The answer is evaluation and cultivation.

Write Everything Down

Putting processes in place to make sure that innovation is expressed to accommodate generational needs is critical to the organization's ongoing success. Processes, however, are of no benefit unless proper systems have been created and chronicled. One of the biggest mistakes organizations make is creating a program without chronicling a system. A system is an organized process that spells out and details specific actions leading to an intended result.

Organizations should utilize the following steps to ensure systems are adequate to maintain a culture of innovative change:

1. **State the name of the process.**

   This is done, primarily, for identification purposes.

2. **State the original intent of the process and its need for innovative change.**

   People need a point of reference so that they understand the spirit in which the change was made.

3. **State the expected results.**

   A change leader should never go into a project without first counting the cost or envisioning the expected result. If anyone needs to know what the expected end will look like, it is the one leading the project. While in most cases that consists of the pastor of a church, or the CEO of a business, other key participants also need to understand what things should look like when all is said and done.

4. **State the key participants.**

   Understanding who participated and why they participated is key to organization makeup, dynamics, execution, and follow-up.

5. **State the steps leading to innovative change.**

   This comprises the critical elements and steps taken to bring the process from vision to fruition. Take the time to include every step, regardless of its importance, including who did what to bring it to conclusion. Identify any missteps that had to be corrected, so that they are not repeated in the future.

6. **State the end result of the project and the benefits it brought.**

   People need to know what the results look like so they can replicate it, or innovate it, should the need arise.

Timeframe of the Project

It is good to give everyone some idea of how long it took to bring the project to completion. This should help them as they prepare for future iterations or new projects.

Review Your Process

The best way to improve on a process and create models of excellence in ministry and business practices is to evaluate every major project presented by the organization. These three questions should always be asked when evaluating a plan, system, or process:

1. **What worked?**

   There will always be successes to your project. Acknowledge and celebrate them and those who accomplished them.

2. **What didn't work?**

   There will almost always be things that either did not work or need improvement. Acknowledge these items, celebrate the effort, and brainstorm better ways to perform the action in the future.

3. **What can be done better?**

   One of the best ways to perpetuate innovative change is to understand that people, projects, plans, systems, and processes can always get better. Find ways to celebrate the efforts of those involved, but always push them to become their better selves.

When these plans, steps, and systems are put into place, they will help to sustain the organization and create an environment and culture of innovation and sustainability.

Chapter Nine

Final Thoughts "Bathed in Prayer"

Be anxious for nothing, but in everything by prayer and supplication, with thanksgiving, let your requests be made known to God; and the peace of God, which surpasses all understanding, will guard your hearts and minds through Christ Jesus.

—Philippians 4:6–7 (NKJV)

I believe I could not have done the things, nor accomplished the projects that I have, both at Grace Church and throughout my ministry, without the discipline of devotion, meditation, and prayer. *Never* underestimate the power of prayer! In my early days as a pastor, I did not understand the power in prayer. Sure, I would pray daily, and I would also pray when I was in preparation for some project or event, and of course before meals and before and after every meeting. But it was not a lifestyle choice. About seven years into my ministry, my whole approach to prayer changed. Before I do anything, each morning, I spend time in prayer and the ministry of the Word. It is my "me time" with the Father. It is the time when He corrects, encourages, enlightens, reveals, assures and guides me into the affairs of my days. Even the writing of this book is divinely inspired by the Spirit of Christ. I take no credit for this: *All* of the glory belongs to Him! And if I had not developed this discipline, I *know* I wouldn't be where I am today.

I challenge you to spend time with the Father. Bathe every decision you make, both personally and professionally, in prayer. Never start your day, start a project, prepare a preaching or teaching assignment, eat a meal, start or end a meeting, enter into a worship service, provide counsel or instruction, or go about your day without it!

If you haven't begun already, now is a great time to start. If you already have begun, continue to grow in your intimate fellowship with Him. I can assure you that He will direct your path and guard your hearts and minds in Christ Jesus!

The pot is in your hands. What will you do with it?

Afterword

*I*t has always been the task of leaders to manage change. For as long as humans have organized themselves into communities, there have been leaders, and there has been change. What is different about the times we live in, however, is the rate of change. The current era is sometimes called "liquid modernity." Structures of society, ways of doing business, cultural values, means of accessing information, and many other aspects of modern life change so rapidly that it can be hard to find one's footing. Leaders in today's world must be able to work within situations of rapid flux.

This has never been clearer than during the COVID-19 pandemic. If this protracted crisis has taught us anything, it is that life is less predictable than we thought. Almost overnight, it seemed, the world was brought to its knees by a virus we did not understand and for which we were unprepared. Our normal patterns of life hit a brick wall. Businesses closed, some of which will never reopen again. Unemployment began to soar. The economy struggled and continues to do so. Large gatherings became "super spreader" events. Even holiday family gatherings were disrupted. Churches have been among the organizations most affected. Gathering, singing, shaking hands, hugging, taking communion—activities common to churches around the world—fell victim to the stigma of this contagion. COVID-19 punctured our illusion of life's predictability. It was incumbent upon leaders to make changes in a way that most of us have not faced in our lifetime.

Drawing upon decades of experience, Dr. Sadler has presented us with the concept of the PotChanger. It may be that in a particular situation, minor changes are in order. The structure and organization in which one locates the problems at hand may be sufficient to contain their remedy, as well. At other times, however, new types of structure and organization are necessary. An organization or structure may simply be outdated. It may lack integrity. It may never have been particularly effective. Or, as in our time, some extraordinary crisis may suddenly render our old paradigms obsolete. In many cases, it will not be enough to make adjustments inside of old structures. We will have to change them, or they will change in spite of us. An effective leader will understand not just the need for change, but the extent to which it is necessary. He or she will be both discerning and adaptive.

Long before "liquid modernity" or COVID-19, Jesus taught, "No one puts new wine into old wineskins".

This world needs Jesus. He is the Way, the Truth, and the Life. And from the earliest days of our faith, leaders have had to adapt to changing circumstances in principled ways in order to lead their communities in faithfulness to Him. Long before "liquid modernity" or COVID-19, Jesus taught, "No one puts new wine into old wineskins" (Mark 2:22 NKJV). Why not? The old wineskins will burst. They have stretched as far as they can. Sometimes minor changes are not enough. We need new paradigms, and we need new leaders who can see when, how, and how much change is required. Christ taught us, though in a different metaphor, that we need PotChangers. Adaptive leadership is not easy work, but it is essential work, and when carried out in service to Christ and His church, it is holy work.

David F. Watson, PhD, academic dean
United Theological Seminary, Dayton, Ohio